REVOLUTION BLUEPRINT

NOT A REVOLUTION OF VIOLENCE, BUT OF LAW, DUTY, AND CONSTITUTIONAL AUTHORITY

THE FOUNDERS GAVE US THE INSTRUCTIONS; THIS IS THE BLUEPRINT TO FOLLOW THEM

BY ROBERT M. IOBBI

A USA Publishing Hub Book

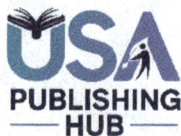

PUBLISHING HUB

Book Title: *Revolution Blueprint*
Author: Robert M. Iobbi

Printed in the United States of America

Book Cover & Book Design by: USA Publishing Hub

CONTENTS

PRELUDE

The Revolution Blueprint is not a call for rebellion, insurrection, or civil war, it is a call to action, a plan to reclaim our government by uniting the people to enforce the principles enshrined in the Constitution. This is not about destruction but restoration. It is a strategy to return liberty to the people and sovereignty to the states, as intended by our founding fathers. This is the path, the only path, to save our constitutional republic. The time for complacency has passed. We stand at a pivotal moment in history, and the future of our nation depends on us. I am just one man with a vision, a plan too big to achieve alone. I'm asking you to join me in this fight for the soul of our nation. I am not a saint or a scholar, nor do I claim to be exceptional in any way except for my love of country. I am a working-class patriot, driven by an unshakable respect for the Constitution and fueled by a passion to see it upheld. Alongside my fellow veterans and patriots, I am prepared to give everything for this mission. This is not about being anti-government; it is about demanding a government that honors the constitutional limits placed upon it, a government of, by, and for the people. The time for action is now. It is a call for the bravest among us to rise, to step forward with resolve and be counted. Your courage, your determination, and your unwavering commitment are needed. Answer the call. Let your bravery inspire others, let it shine as a beacon of hope for your family, your community, and your country. Together, we will restore the Constitution. Together, we will save our republic.

"If there must be trouble, let it be in my day, that my child may may have peace, and this single reflection, well applied, is sufficient to awaken every man to his duty." Revolutionary - Thomas Paine

REVOLUTION BLUEPRINT

1

THE STATE OF OUR UNION

I n the beginning, we were a nation united by the most sought-after principle throughout all of history: Liberty. Tragically, the country we inhabit today starkly contrasts with the vision of our founding fathers. In 1776, our nation declared independence from the oppressive rule of Great Britain, and during the Revolutionary War, 25,000 patriots sacrificed their lives for liberty.

Unity was the foundation of our victory and the birth of the greatest nation on Earth. United, we stood and conquered an empire. Today, divided, we are being conquered. A nation divided against itself cannot stand; it collapses under tyranny. And today, The United States of America is collapsing before our eyes.

Although a relatively young nation, America once stood as a beacon of hope, a guiding light for those yearning for freedom. We were united in our belief in greatness and pursued it with unwavering determination. Today, however, that unity has fractured, and our greatness is slipping away. For decades, politicians from both the Democratic and Republican parties have enacted policies that enable the exploitation of our nation by central bankers and foreign adversaries, depleting our resources and eroding our liberties to satisfy their insatiable greed. Yet the blame does not rest solely on the corrupt political parties. We, the people, have contributed to this decline by allowing ourselves to remain divided and distracted, losing sight of the principles that once bound us together. When we examine the current State of our Union, it becomes clear that we are a nation accelerating toward its own demise. The years of reckless abandonment of border security, coupled with a relentless addiction to unchecked government spending, standing as the most significant threat to our nation's future. The national debt crisis we face today is not the result of centuries of accumulated spending but is directly tied to policy failures and political corruption over the past thirty years. Under the leadership of George W. Bush and Barack Hussein Obama, the United States government was fundamentally transformed into a bloated and overreaching unelected bureaucracy. During these administrations, the national debt skyrocketed, the size and scope of government bureaucracy massively expanded unchecked, and individual liberties were severely contracted. Consider the consequences of the people's complacency. Unsecured borders have permitted millions of fighting-age males from across the globe to enter our country unchecked, creating significant security and social challenges. At the same time, Mexican drug cartels have flooded our communities with deadly narcotics such as heroin, cocaine, and fentanyl, exacerbating the crisis. Compounding this tragedy, the Food and Drug Administration (FDA), in collaboration with pharmaceutical companies, has enabled the rampant overprescription of opioids, resulting in a devastating addiction epidemic that has torn apart countless families and communities throughout the nation. The Centers for Disease Control (CDC) and the National Institute of Allergy and Infectious Diseases (NIAID), in coordination with both domestic and foreign bad actors, worsened domestic suffering during the COVID-19 pandemic. Their actions prioritized a globalist agenda and the promotion of experimental vaccines, resulting in significant erosion of public trust. These efforts, which ultimately enriched their institutions and affiliates with billions in profits, came at the cost of countless lives, all while being financed by the hard-earned dollars of American taxpayers. The Environmental Protection Agency (EPA) has imposed overbearing regulations that suffocate energy production causing inflation of all goods and services hindering economic growth. Our brave servicemen and women are continually sent to fight wars that have no bearing on our national security or freedoms, serving instead the greed of political leaders and the ideological ambitions of a globalist agenda. These systemic failures underscore how our government has drifted far from its intended purpose, prioritizing power, profit, and control over the welfare and liberty of its citizens. When we reflect on our national debt, now exceeding $36 trillion, and a bloated government spending over $7 trillion annually with no accountability, it becomes clear that decades of unchecked corruption in spending is fueling hyperinflation, draining resources from millions of struggling families, exacerbating the decline of the middle class and contributing to the growing homeless crisis. This decline is further compounded by failing school systems in deteriorating cities, the ongoing systemic oppression of Black Americans, the collapse of manufacturing industries, a weakened labor market, and the growth of a welfare state that provides sustenance but no clear path to self-sufficiency or prosperity. Yet, amid these challenges, the ultimate responsibility lies with us, the citizens of this nation, voters and non-voters alike. We allow ourselves to be divided into partisan camps of Republicans and Democrats, clinging to party loyalty with blind allegiance. In doing so, we fail to see that this unwavering loyalty to political parties betrays our country and its core values. Our partisanship not only deepens division but also fuels the corruption that continues to permeate our government with absolute impunity. Our Founding Fathers displayed unparalleled genius in their design of our constitutional republic, embedding safeguards to preserve liberty and limit the overreach of power. Among their most urgent warnings was the danger of political alliances, alliances that could undermine the very foundation of the republic. Tragically, this precise threat has brought our nation to the brink of collapse. The hyper-partisan nature of modern government, fueled by billions of dollars spent each election cycle to secure power, lies at the core of nearly every issue plaguing our country. The Democratic and Republican parties have weaponized their alliances to dominate federal, state, and local governments, seizing control of our entire republic. Through laws, policies, and regulations designed to fortify their stronghold, they have expanded government power well beyond the limits set forth in the United States Constitution.

This overreach stands in direct violation of the agreement between the states that established the federal government. Yet, the states have failed to resist the federal government's encroachment on their sovereignty because the same political parties controlling Washington also control every political office within state governments. This consolidation of power is the very definition of tyranny, the exact form of oppression our Founding Fathers warned us to guard against. The Democratic and Republican parties have become the architects of the system they were meant to prevent. Political alliances have deeply entrenched themselves within the electorate, creating an environment of extreme division. It is increasingly evident that we no longer vote for the best candidates; instead, our primary motivation is often to prevent the opposing party's candidate from winning. Many of us recognize this unsettling reality, we have lost confidence in the parties that claim to represent our values, yet we feel trapped by the belief that supporting an alternative might enable the "greater evil" to prevail. This has reduced our elections to a disheartening "hold your nose and vote" exercise, where individual causes often take precedence over the unified greatness of the nation. We can point fingers at one party or the other, but the undeniable truth is that both parties have jointly governed this nation for the past century, each taking turns wielding power. And during that time, both have contributed equally to the systemic failures that plague us today. The two-party system has proven itself incapable of solving the nation's problems; in fact, it has been the driving force behind many of them. Both parties have voted to tax nearly every aspect of our lives, our labor, commerce, property, farms, and even our estates after death, while simultaneously wasting trillions of taxpayer dollars on policies and budgets that expand government far beyond its constitutional limits. Both parties voted for policies that crippled domestic manufacturing, shipping our good jobs overseas, all with the intent of shrinking our middle class and weakening our dollar. The two parties also share responsibility for disastrous decisions, such as the deregulation of mortgage-backed securities that contributed to the 21st-century economic recession. Many of their members personally profited from reckless lending practices, which devastated institutions like Fannie Mae and Freddie Mac and drained trillions of dollars in wealth and land equity from the middle class. Adding insult to injury, they then over-regulated the banking industry, while the Federal Reserve hiked consumer rates, exacerbating the crisis. When the housing bubble inevitably burst, Congress voted to use taxpayer dollars to bail out the very same reckless banks and lending institutions that caused the collapse. Not one banker or public official responsible for this corruption was held accountable. Instead, the burden of their greed was shifted onto hardworking Americans, further eroding trust in our institutions. This bipartisan pattern of self-interest, mismanagement, and corruption underscores a painful reality: the two-party system has failed the American people. It continues to prioritize power and profit over accountability and the well-being of the nation. The harm inflicted upon this nation by these two self-serving political parties is undeniable. Their actions make it abundantly clear that their loyalty lies not with the American people, but with their own interests and those of their corporate benefactors. They have shown little regard for the well-being of the country or its citizens, prioritizing power and profit over responsible governance. This reckless abandonment of good leadership must end. It is time for "We the People" to confront a critical question: Are we truly willing to mortgage the future of our children and grandchildren by continuing our allegiance to these two corrupt political parties as they repeatedly betray our nation to central banks and globalist agendas? Will we remain divided as Democrats and Republicans, or will we rise together as Americans to dismantle the stranglehold of this two-party monopoly that is corroding our republic? We must recognize a fundamental truth:

nowhere in the Constitution are political parties granted power or authority to control our government or its functions. Their self-appointed dominance is a usurpation of the people's power, and it is within our rights to take it back. The time has come to reclaim the government for the people, by the people, and demand accountability from those who have long abandoned their duty to serve the nation. Make no mistake, the challenge before us is extreme, but so was the fight for independence from the British Empire. History has shown that great change requires great determination. The most crucial truth we must accept is this: to solve our nation's problems, we must first remove those in power who actively obstruct their resolution. Politicians and public officials who have violated their sworn oaths to uphold the Constitution, betraying the people they were elected to serve by aligning themselves with lobbyists, special interests, and foreign adversaries, have forfeited their right to hold office. These individuals, having put personal gain above the public good, have disqualified themselves from public service and must be removed from the hallowed positions of government they have disgraced, saving of our republic depends on it. The Revolution Blueprint offers a straightforward yet pragmatic plan to peacefully reclaim our government and restore the United States to its rightful place as a free republic, governed strictly within the limits established by our great Constitution. The obstacles to our nation's greatness have never been clearer, and neither have the identities of those who benefit from the dysfunction. For them, America is not broken; it is a system working exactly as intended, enabling them to accumulate immense wealth and power at the expense of hardworking men and women across the country. These politicians are loyal only to their political parties and wealthy donors, donors who fund their campaigns and, in return, are rewarded with lucrative government contracts, grants, loans, and tax breaks once their "bought and paid for" candidates are elected. This unholy alliance is further fortified by a complicit and corrupt media, controlled by the same central bankers who own the politicians. Together, they form the establishment class, a powerful elite that prioritizes self-interest and greed over the well-being of the nation. It is this establishment that is systematically eroding the foundations of America, and it is this establishment that must be confronted if we are to save the republic. Let there be no misunderstanding; this deep state bureaucracy stands as the primary obstacle to saving our republic and is the true enemy of our freedoms. Should our movement to restore the republic gain momentum among the people, we can expect the establishment to respond with fierce opposition. They will attack us from all sides, labeling us radicals and falsely claiming that we pose the greatest threat to our democracy. But understand this: what the establishment fears most is a unified citizenry acting in our powers. We, the people, are the ultimate authority, and it is our collective will that determines their existence. Challenging a corrupt system comes with significant risks. Any individual who dares to rise against this entrenched power does so at great peril to their freedom and well-being. The treatment of the January 6th protesters serves as a stark reminder of the high stakes involved when confronting tyranny. Yet, as citizens of this once revered nation, we must find the courage to stand firm. We must remind those we elect that they are public servants, accountable to the people. The true power in this republic resides not in the hands of the politicians but in the hands of the people and it is time we reclaim it. Those clinging to their stranglehold on power over our nation understand precisely what is at stake if the people were to unite against them, vast wealth, unchecked authority, and the consequences of their actions. They fear losing it all. Meanwhile, tens of millions of Americans are increasingly fed up, deeply frustrated, and disgusted by the deliberate dismantling of our country. We are tired of watching the Constitution, the very foundation of our republic, being twisted and perverted by the same representatives sworn to uphold and defend it. Despite our anger and disillusionment, we often remain uninformed about the extent of the corruption embedded in the laws and policies being enacted. The waste and mismanagement of taxpayer dollars have driven our nation to the brink of financial ruin, yet we have made little effort to confront or stop those responsible. Complacency has been our greatest weakness, and it has gone on for far too long. The time has come for the people to rise, to unite against tyranny, and to reclaim the principles and freedoms that have been stolen from us. Only through collective action can we restore our nation to its former greatness. I deeply believe in the principles upon which our government was founded, principles rooted in liberty, justice, and representation. I believe in the government we were meant to have, not the unconstitutional, overreaching entity that governs us today. Regardless of its size, there is a fundamental difference between the limited government envisioned by our Founding Fathers and the bloated, self-serving structure now in place. This current government no longer represents the people; it serves cronies, special interests, and foreign adversaries wealthy enough to buy influence and shape policy to their advantage. I also believe in learning from our nation's rich history. What I propose is not a regression to the 18th century but a return to a government that fully and faithfully adheres to the Constitution, without exception or compromise. It is my hope that we can set aside our divisions as Democrats and Republicans and unite as patriots, just as our Founding Fathers once did, to rebuild a truly indivisible nation. The effort to reclaim our government must be conducted in a manner consistent with the Constitution. We must honor the processes and principles enshrined in our founding documents. This is the only path to restoring our constitutional republic and securing a future we can be proud to leave for our children.

I envision a future where government waste and reckless spending are eliminated, and the federal debt no longer cripples our economy. Poverty is rare, homelessness is eradicated, and opportunity abounds for all. Manufacturing and technology flourish, creating high paying jobs and upward mobility for millions of Americans. Workers retain the full fruits of their labor, free from excessive taxation. The Family unit is strengthened, and the poor are empowered through education and training. Our racial divides are bridged, and we finally move past the sins of our nation's history, liberating Black Americans from centuries of systemic oppression.

My vision is one that restores the fundamental opportunities our Founding Fathers declared for us: the rights to life, liberty, and the pursuit of happiness. Let every American choose their happiness and pursue it freely. At the heart of every issue we face is one undeniable truth: the people have lost control of their government. Public officials who swear an oath to uphold the Constitution are openly and brazenly violating its terms. This is the crux of our nation's struggles, and until we reclaim that control, true reform will remain out of reach. The time to act is now. We must restore our government to one that serves its people, honors its Constitution, and ensures the promise of freedom and opportunity for generations to come. The Revolution Blueprint outlines a clear and constitutional plan for the people to reclaim control of our government by enforcing Article VI, Clause III of the Constitution. Under its provisions, any public official, elected or appointed, who has openly violated their sworn oath to uphold the Constitution is disqualified from public service. These individuals must face immediate removal from public office, without exception. Furthermore, those found guilty of corruption or treason will be held accountable through appropriate legal actions, including arrest. In their place, a new government, of the people, by the people, and for the people, will be established. Individuals sworn into vacated offices will take the America First Pledge, committing themselves to the full restoration of constitutional governance. This government will uphold the rule of law, ensure justice is served to all who deserve it, and hold every traitor accountable for their criminal and unconstitutional acts against the nation.

This blueprint is a call to action for accountability, integrity, and the re-establishment of the true republic government that honors its founding principles and serves its people. The Revolution Blueprint provides compelling evidence that Obamacare is unconstitutional and exceeds the federal government's taxing powers. Described as one of the most significant legislative frauds ever imposed on the American people, Obamacare represents an overreach that undermines constitutional principles. The Blueprint outlines a plan to repeal this legislation and replace it with a more practical, affordable, and sustainable free-market healthcare system. This approach ensures healthcare is managed at the state level, utilizing state healthcare agencies and fully removing the federal government's unlawful role in the nation's healthcare system. Additionally, the Blueprint proposes a balanced plan to address illegal immigration with both vigilance and compassion. Decades of inaction and poor border policies have created a complex crisis requiring decisive action. The unchecked influx of millions of fighting-age males into the country necessitates a robust and vigilant effort to restore border integrity and remove those who have entered illegally. At the same time, compassion must be extended to families who have integrated into American communities over the years, recognizing the need for fair and humane solutions. This two-pronged approach seeks to restore law and order while honoring our values as a nation. While my views and opinions may not be the ultimate authority on these issues, I strongly believe that logical solutions exist to bridge our divides and find common ground. When we take a step back to examine the roots of our division, the motives of those who seek to keep us fragmented become strikingly clear. In this light, it becomes evident that many of the disagreements dividing us are far less significant than they appear, especially when stripped of the media's relentless efforts to inflame and manipulate those differences.

The Revolution Blueprint is rooted in a nonpartisan mission to reclaim our government from the corrupt, entrenched class that is eroding America from within. Our aim is simple: to restore our nation to a constitutional republic, that faithfully adheres to the principles and boundaries set forth in our founding documents. This is not about left or right, it is about putting America back on a path of integrity, unity, and liberty. I deeply love my country, and I believe that same unwavering patriotism lives on in the hearts and minds of the vast majority of Americans. It is this shared love for our great nation that will unite us in our mission to reclaim our government from the grip of tyranny. Our greatest strength lies in our unity, for a united body of citizens is unstoppable. With determination and collective resolve, we can Raise the Republic to its rightful place as a beacon of hope and a shining symbol of freedom for the entire world. God bless America and our mission to rebuild and restore her greatness.

CONSTITUTION ENFORCEMENT

In the midst of our republic's rapid decline, the wisdom of our nation's first president echoes louder than ever. In his 1796 Farewell Address, George Washington warned: "However [political parties] may now and then answer popular ends, they are likely in the course of time and things, to become potent engines, by which cunning, ambitious, and unprincipled men will be enabled to subvert the power of the people and to usurp for themselves the reins of government, destroying afterwards the very engines which have lifted them to unjust dominion." Today, we are living in the shadow of those prophetic words. The Democrat and Republican parties, once mere instruments of representation, have seized the reins of government for their own gain, betraying the very principles that elevated them. These privately controlled entities now pose the greatest threat to the survival of our republic, embodying the very "domestic enemy" against which the fighting men and women of this great nation have sworn an oath to protect and defend against. Instead of serving the people, those we elect and appoint to the offices of our governments have pledged their allegiance to these political machines, prioritizing party agendas over their solemn duty to the Constitution. This betrayal stands in direct violation of Article VI, Clause III, which clearly mandates: "The Senators and Representatives before mentioned, and the Members of the several State Legislatures, and all executive and Judicial Officers, both of the United States and of the several States, shall be bound by Oath or Affirmation, to support this Constitution." It is this breach of duty, this subversion of our foundational principles, that demands our immediate attention and action. The enforcement of the Constitution is no longer just a duty, it is the only means to restore the integrity of our republic and preserve the liberties we hold dear.

The Constitution is, at its core, a binding contract among the several states that established the federal government of the United States. Through this contract, specific powers are enumerated and granted to the federal government within its articles. The 10th Amendment exists as a safeguard, ensuring the sovereignty of the states and the rights of the people by strictly limiting federal authority to those powers explicitly delegated to it by the Constitution. Any powers not granted to the federal government, nor prohibited to the states, are reserved to the states respectively, or to the people. Yet, cunning and unprincipled members of both the Democratic and Republican parties have conspired to violate this foundational contract. Despite swearing an oath or affirming their commitment to uphold the Constitution, they have relentlessly expanded the government's powers far beyond its constitutional limits. This has given rise to a bureaucratic monstrosity, Permanent Washington, a sprawling, unaccountable system that even its creators cannot control. Every manifestation of tyranny in our nation stems from this systemic failure. Politicians and unelected officials have repeatedly disregarded the Constitution's limits, undermining the very principles they are bound to uphold. All who serve at the federal and state levels of government are sworn to support and defend the Constitution, yet violations of its terms persist at every level. To restore liberty and accountability, we must demand adherence to the Constitution, not as a suggestion, but as the supreme law of the land. Without enforcement of this contract, the very fabric of our republic will continue to unravel.

A Nation Under Siege

Our nation is enduring immense suffering, facing crises on multiple fronts, but none is more critical or dire than the illegal immigration crisis. The United States has been invaded, and the Constitution explicitly requires the United States Government to protect the states from such an invasion. The government's failure to fulfill this duty represents one of the most blatant and egregious violations of the Constitution. Worse, this failure is no accident. It is a deliberate act, a betrayal of the states and the people they are sworn to serve. By purposefully allowing and even facilitating this invasion, the government has committed an act of treason against the nation. The absence of accountability is an even greater treachery that cannot and must not be tolerated any longer. For the American people, there is only one course of action if we are to save our country: the terms of the Constitution must be enforced in their entirety, without exceptions, and with the utmost urgency. Our republic cannot endure if its foundational laws are ignored. The time to act is now, and the stakes could not be higher.

The Surrender of the United States to Globalism

The United States of America has been handed over to the globalist agenda of a one-world government, fundamentally transforming our republic into a communist regime. The architects of Permanent Washington, a cabal of unelected bureaucrats, surrendered this nation to globalism on September 11, 2001. The corporation through its figure heads, such as George Bush, Barack Obama, Hillary Clinton, Joe Biden, and their allies, have aligned our government with the World Economic Forum's agenda, serving interests that undermine American sovereignty. This betrayal is no accident. The long chain of constitutional abuses, the weaponization of government, the manipulation of elections, and the propagation of state-controlled media narratives have all been deliberate. These actions are carefully designed to disarm and divide American patriots, hindering their ability to unite and defend our republic against this orchestrated globalist takeover. Our founding fathers foresaw the dangers of political alliances that would enable cunning and unprincipled individuals to subvert the power of the people and seize control of the government. They warned future generations of this threat, recognizing it as the greatest danger to our republic's survival. To protect against such tyranny, they established a system of government with four critical fail-safe mechanisms, they provided the tools necessary to defend the Constitution and preserve the republic from those who would seek its destruction.

The Constitution provides four methods to enforce its terms and protect the republic from tyranny. However, each has been undermined by systemic corruption, leaving the nation in a precarious state.

The Judiciary

The judiciary is intended as the first line of defense against unconstitutional overreach. Courts have the power to strike down violations of the Constitution and restore its authority. This requires public officials, bound by their oath, to challenge acts of overreach.

The Barrier: Public officials rarely bring these challenges because they are compromised by the same political alliances controlling the government's overreach. While citizens have the right to challenge unconstitutional acts, the cost of legal battles makes this impractical for most. Even when challenges are brought, the judiciary itself is just as deeply compromised by political affiliations and biases, rendering it incapable of impartial judgment. The judiciary has devolved into a broken institution, riddled with conflicts of interest and allegiance to political factions.

Elections

Elections are the most obvious solution: elect representatives who will honor their oaths and uphold the Constitution. The Barrier: Elections in the United States are no longer conducted in a constitutional, legal, or ethical manner. Rampant fraud, irregularities, and even treasonous actions are being used to manipulate outcomes and deny the people's voice. The electoral process is compromised at every level, making it increasingly difficult for patriots to reclaim government through the ballot box.

Convention of the States

State-led intervention, through an Article V Convention of the States, is a powerful constitutional mechanism to enforce the Constitution and counter federal overreach. This process allows states to propose amendments that restore constitutional governance. It requires 34 state legislatures to call for a convention and 38 legislatures to ratify proposed amendments from convention.

The Barrier: State legislatures, like federal officials, are compromised by allegiances to the same two political parties responsible for the overreach. This conflict of interest undermines their ability to act in defense of the Constitution. While the movement for a Convention of the States has made significant progress over the past decade, achieving the required 34 states is highly unlikely in the current political climate. It would require the cooperation of several deep-blue states, which are unlikely to support a convention aimed at curbing federal overreach. Furthermore, the harsh reality is that time is not on our side. The republic is at the brink of collapse, and the luxury of waiting years for political processes to play out no longer exists. The time for trusting politicians and the political process has expired.

The People

The ultimate power to enforce the Constitution and dispel tyranny lies with the people, as affirmed in the Declaration of Independence. It is the people who hold absolute authority over all governments, and it is their right and duty to act when all other mechanisms fail.

The Resolve: The founding fathers designed the system to place the ultimate responsibility on the people to defend liberty. When the judiciary is compromised, elections are corrupted, and the states fail to act, it is the people who must rise, unite, and restore the republic. Time is of the essence, and the survival of our nation depends on immediate and decisive action. The Constitution belongs to the people, and it is through their courage and determination that the republic can be saved.

The people's declaration of power

"We hold these truths to be self-evident, that all men are created equal, that they are endowed by their creator with certain unalienable rights, that among these are life, liberty, and the pursuit of happiness. That to secure these rights, governments are instituted amongst men deriving their just powers from the consent of the governed, that whenever any form of government becomes destructive to these ends, it is the right of the people to alter or abolish it." The Founding Fathers shared their wisdom on the People's Inalienable Rights and Power to Alter Government.

"When once a Republic is corrupted, there is no possibility of remedying any of the growing evils but by removing the corruption and restoring its lost principles."

"The people alone have an incontestable, unalienable, and indefeasible right to institute government, and to reform, alter, or completely change it, whenever their protection, safety, prosperity, and happiness demand it."

These words from the founding fathers serve as a timeless reminder: the power to shape, restore, and, if necessary, rebuild government lies solely with the people. When corruption takes root, and the principles of liberty are lost, it is not just the right but the duty of the people to act. Only through their resolve can a nation reclaim its foundation and secure the freedoms essential to its survival.

The People's Power to Defend the Republic

The Declaration of Independence firmly establishes the absolute power of the people over their government. The Second Amendment reinforces this by providing the means to defend and protect that power:

"A well-regulated Militia, being necessary to the security of a free state, the right of the people to keep and bear arms, shall not be infringed."

The Constitutional Crisis

The long chain of government overreach and constitutional abuse persists because the government no longer fears the people. Without accountability, tyranny thrives, and the principles of liberty and justice are trampled underfoot.

The People's Resolution

To reclaim the government and enforce the terms of the Constitution, the people must organize and unite, building a coalition of patriots to serve as an acting well-regulated militia, one million strong and united in the cause of liberty, is the only way to restore balance and reassert the people's sovereignty. A unified and prepared militia is the one thing tyrants fear most. The government and its media apparatus would have you believe that such constitutional action amounts to insurrection or even civil war. In reality, it is the government itself that is sewing division and chaos, intentionally driving citizens against one another to ignite a civil war amongst ourselves. A divided citizenry will never stand united, and this is precisely what those in power desire, a weakened, fragmented population incapable of resistance.

The Revolution Blueprint

What follows is The Revolution Blueprint, a comprehensive plan for reclaiming our public offices, sitting down the central bank, corporations, and foreign adversaries controlling our governments and ending the long chain of constitutional abuses. Rooted in the methodology of the founding fathers in 1776, this Blueprint declares the causes for intervention and outlines a constitutional path to peacefully restore the Republic. It begins by enforcing Article VI, Clause III of the Constitution:

"The Senators and Representatives before mentioned, and the Members of the several State Legislatures, and all executive and Judicial Officers, both of the United States and of the several States, shall be bound by Oath or Affirmation, to support this Constitution." Any public official who violates their sworn oath to support the Constitution is disqualified from serving in public office and must be removed by resignation or termination. The Revolution Blueprint is not a call to arms for conflict but a plan for peace through strength. It seeks to prevent civil war by restoring constitutional order, protecting state sovereignty, and abolishing tyranny from government. It is the founding fathers' instruction manual for safeguarding liberty and ensuring that government operates within the limits placed upon it by the Constitution. The America First pledge lays the foundation for a new government, one built upon principles that respect the people's rights and adhere to constitutional constraints. A government of the people, by the people, and for the people must ultimately be policed by the people. It is the People's Republic. It is the People's Government. It is the People's Power. And it is the People's Civic Duty to Intervene. God Bless America and the Patriots who rise to defend her

The Call to Action

Dark times are upon us, and the survival of our republic hangs in the balance. Patriotism must ignite within the hearts of the bravest among us. It is time for "We the People" to unite and form a coalition, not as an act of war, but as the ultimate act of peace through strength. A united people is the only force capable of protecting this nation from civil war and halting the globalist agenda of Permanent Washington.

RECLAIMING OUR GOVERNMENT

To my fellow patriots who still believe in the Constitution and our inalienable right to liberty, endowed by our creator, this message is addressed to you with the utmost urgency. The gravity of our nation's predicament demands swift and decisive action.

The time for idly complaining without a clear plan for resolution has passed. The United States government has become undeniably corrupt, hollowed out by tyranny, and unrecognizable in its betrayal of the people it was established to serve. For far too long, it has operated against the interests of the nation and its citizenry. As citizens of this great nation, we are the rightful masters of our government. Yet, we have faltered in our sacred duty to hold our public officials accountable to their oaths of office. Article VI, Clause 3 of the Constitution explicitly requires all elected officials and appointed bureaucrats to swear an oath to support and uphold the Constitution:

"The Senators and Representatives before mentioned, and the Members of the several State Legislatures, and all executive and judicial officers, both of the United States and of the several States, shall be bound by Oath or Affirmation, to support this Constitution."

The oath or affirmation is not a mere formality, it is a binding commitment to honor and protect the principles that uphold our republic. Yet, that commitment has been repeatedly and systematically violated, leaving the people to bear the consequences of unchecked tyranny. The time has come to reclaim our government. It is our civic duty to restore accountability, enforce the Constitution, and reassert the sovereignty of "We the People." The survival of our nation depends on it.

The Betrayal of America: A Corrupt System in Crisis

Few members of the Republican and Democratic parties truly uphold the Constitution as their oath of office demands. None faithfully discharge their duties in a way that protects and honors the principles enshrined in our founding document. Even those who do respect their oaths find themselves powerless, hamstrung by the bureaucratic stranglehold these political parties exert over the legislative process. The Republican and Democratic parties have hijacked our government, transforming it into a corrupt machine operating neither efficiently nor constitutionally. The laws of this nation are no longer faithfully executed. Political offices are openly sold to special interests and foreign adversaries, with Congress brazenly disregarding its constitutional and statutory responsibilities. For over 20 years, since 2005, Congress has failed to deliberate the 12 appropriations of federal spending as required by law. They have completely ignored their obligation to pass a balanced budget, opting instead for "continuing resolutions" stuffed with unnecessary and wasteful spending. This blatant disregard for their oath and duties has led to a staggering increase in the national debt, which has ballooned from $7 trillion to over $36 trillion in just twenty years. In just a three-year span of time, the federal government spent a staggering $20.3 trillion, with annual deficits now averaging near $2 trillion. To put this into perspective, federal spending nearly doubles the spending of all state and local governments combined. Compounding this fiscal crisis is the persistent presence of over $3 trillion in nonessential and wasteful spending embedded in each federal budget. These expenditures, rather than being scrutinized and reduced, are automatically renewed every year 7% with baseline budgeting increase, an inflationary growth that Congress has refused to address or deliberate upon. This reckless pattern of spending showcases a dire lack of fiscal accountability, burdening taxpayers while neglecting critical priorities. Instead of responsible governance, this unchecked waste exacerbates the national debt, destabilizes the economy, and diverts resources from investments that could uplift communities, repair infrastructure, and strengthen the nation. This trajectory is unsustainable, irresponsible, and a direct affront to the principles of fiscal discipline and accountability that should guide our government. It is imperative for Congress to prioritize transparency, deliberate over budgets, and eliminate the inefficiencies that jeopardize the financial future of the nation. Adding insult to injury, the government has engaged in a multi-trillion-dollar foreign aid money-laundering scheme during these same two decades. This practice, which is unconstitutional, funnels American taxpayer dollars to foreign nations while neglecting our own. Congress has no constitutional authority to spend taxpayer money on foreign nations, yet it does so regularly. Imagine the transformative power of reallocating just $50 billion annually from foreign aid to revitalize America's decaying cities. In just a few short years, 50 distressed cities could be renewed, creating jobs, improving infrastructure, and uplifting struggling communities. Yet instead, hundreds of billions of dollars are sent overseas or allocated to supporting foreigners entering our country illegally.

Who pays the price?

Black Americans, in particular, should be outraged. These funds could end generational systemic oppression, rebuild neglected communities, and provide critical resources to uplift citizens through education and new opportunities. Yet the government chooses to prioritize foreign nations over its own citizens.

Why has our government spent more than $10 trillion dollars abroad? Because when taxpayer money is funneled overseas, it can be laundered back into the pockets of corrupt politicians and their special interests. Foreign aid has become a lucrative scheme, enriching career politicians who earn $200,000 per year in government salaries yet amass millions in personal wealth. This corruption extends beyond foreign aid. Over the past three decades, both parties have engineered trade policies and tax codes that favor foreign nations at the expense of American manufacturing.

Millions of high-paying jobs have been lost, leaving communities in ruins. Meanwhile, these same politicians profit from the foreign corporations that fill the manufacturing void, holding stocks and securing lucrative board positions for their families in the very companies benefitting from America's decline. This is the essence of claims that "China owns our politicians." China's strategy to weaken the United States is simple: buy off our corrupt leaders, whose self-serving culture makes them easy targets. This treasonous behavior has devastated our economy and hollowed out our nation's industrial base.

The Hard Truth: Elections Alone Won't Fix This

The institutional power of the corporation controlling all governments and manipulating policies through these two parties is so pervasive that placing hope in elections is the definition of insanity. Time and again, we replace corrupt politicians with good Americans, only to see them swallowed up by the monstrous bureaucracy of Permanent Washington. No election alone will dismantle this system. The bureaucracy, corruption, and collusion that have overtaken our government must be confronted directly. It is not just about electing better representatives; it is about reclaiming the government, enforcing the Constitution, and uprooting the entrenched systems that have betrayed the American people.

The time for half-measures has passed. If we are to restore our republic, bold, decisive action is required. Only then can we free ourselves from the grip of the corporation and rebuild a government that truly serves the people.

The Fight Against America First

The entrenched political elites, both Republican and Democrat, opposed President Trump's "America First" agenda because it threatened their corrupt system. They weaponized the CIA, FBI, DOJ, and judiciary against Trump's presidency and reelection campaign to protect their interests.

The Bulletproof Corruption of Government

The stranglehold the two-party system has over our government is impervious to elections. This corruption is deeply embedded in the policies implemented over decades, especially in the aftermath of the orchestrated attacks on 9/11. That event became the catalyst for a massive expansion of government power and an accelerated erosion of our liberties. For many, it marked the moment our government surrendered the United States to globalist control.

The globalist-driven political class has achieved exactly what they set out to do: fundamentally transform the way our system of government operates. The institutional power of the two-party system cannot and will not be defeated by electing representatives from either the Republican or Democratic parties. These two entities are the architects of every failure and crisis we face today. It is not a complex problem to understand, every issue plaguing this nation can be traced back to decisions made by these two corrupt parties. Yet, we continue to place hope in a broken system, expecting change from the very institutions responsible for our suffering. This reliance on corrupt elections spanning over 50 years has been a failed strategy that our nation cannot afford to pursue any longer. We are hurtling toward disaster on a runaway train, and the bridge ahead is out. This is no longer a matter of debate or political preference; it is an undeniable truth we must face immediately. If we fail to unite and reclaim our government from the two-party system that is systematically destroying our country from within, America as we know it will fall. We are dangerously close to that collapse. Yet, the war is not lost. There is still time to save our great nation. But saving it requires action, bold, decisive action from brave Americans who are united in their mission. We must stand together, united in purpose, united in our vision for the future, and united in our plan to achieve it. To those who dismiss this message as extreme, consider the reality: the dangers threatening our nation are far more extreme. The freedoms we once took for granted in a free America are already gone. The government exploited a pandemic to strip us of our liberties, undermine the presidency, and completely compromise the integrity of our elections. The bureaucratic elites have fundamentally transformed our republic into something unrecognizable. Yes, this is a call to extreme resolve, because nothing less will suffice. The time has come for patriots to confront this domestic enemy with courage, unity, and purpose. It is time to take our country back from these criminals and hold them accountable for their crimes against our nation and humanity. The stakes have never been higher, the time for action is now.

Understanding Our Mission: A Return to Foundational Principles

To understand our mission, we must first grasp its genesis. The Founding Fathers were principled men who, in seeking liberation for their country, believed it essential to clearly declare to a corrupt governing body the reasons for its termination. Their words, etched into history, serve as a timeless guide for addressing tyranny:

"When in the course of human events, it becomes necessary for one people to dissolve the political bands which have connected them with another, and to assume among the powers of the earth, the separate and equal station to which the laws of nature and nature's God entitle them, a decent respect to the opinions of mankind requires that they should declare the causes which impel them to the separation."

For over a century, from the 20th century to today, the Republican and Democratic parties have occupied and controlled every level of our government: local, state, and federal. These two private owned corporations have willfully seized power, hijacking our entire political system for their own gain. In doing so, they have become the sole architects of every failed policy, every act of corruption, and every betrayal of the public trust within our government. Their incompetence, corruption, and negligence reached an undeniable breaking point on September 11, 2001, when it became clear that the government no longer served the national security interests of the United States or its people. In the decades since, this betrayal has only deepened. The failures of the Democratic and Republican parties have left our nation in a state of profound suffering, plagued by corruption, mismanagement, and a disregard for the Constitution. This 100-year streak of treasonous actions and systemic corruption must end now. The people must rise to remove and expel the Democratic and Republican parties from all government offices. Furthermore, their affiliation and influence must be forbidden across every level of governance throughout the United States, ensuring these entities can never again corrupt our republic. This is not just our right; it is our patriotic duty. The Declaration of Independence declares that when a government becomes destructive and tyrannical, the people have both the authority and the obligation to abolish it and replace it with one that prioritizes the well-being of its citizens and adheres to the limits set by the Constitution. It is time to fulfill this duty. We must establish a new government, one that respects the principles of liberty, accountability, and constitutional governance. A government of, by, and for the people must be reclaimed and rebuilt, for the survival of our republic depends on it.

Causation for The People's Intervention:

Failure to Secure the Border and Protect National Sovereignty

The failure to secure our southern border and enforce our nation's immigration laws has resulted in an estimated 30-40 million undocumented individuals living illegally within the United States. For over three decades, the Democratic and Republican parties have prioritized special interests and political agendas over the safety and well-being of American citizens. This neglect has inflicted harm not only on Americans but also on the undocumented individuals crossing the border and living in vulnerable conditions. The financial burden of this failure exceeds hundreds of billions of dollars annually, resources that could and should be directed toward addressing the needs of American citizens. The Constitution delegates limited powers to the federal government to represent the interests of the United States and its citizenry, not those of foreign nations or noncitizens. By failing to secure our borders and uphold immigration laws, our government has demonstrated a gross dereliction of duty and a direct violation of the oaths of office sworn by its members. Surrendering our borders is not merely incompetence, it is treason.

Failure to Execute Responsible Fiscal Policy

For over three decades, Congress has recklessly abandoned its budgeting responsibilities, resulting in a national debt exceeding $36 trillion and at least $20 trillion squandered through fraud, corruption, and waste. The Democratic and Republican parties have spent trillions of taxpayer dollars on wars, special interests, and expenditures that do not serve America's best interests. Meanwhile, states and citizens are starved of resources to address critical challenges. Once-thriving industrial towns and urban centers across the nation are in decay. Homelessness is an epidemic in every state. Schools are failing, infrastructure is crumbling, un-American policies have stripped Americans of well-paying manufacturing jobs, devastated communities and eroded the backbone of our nation's workforce. These misguided decisions have prioritized corporate profits and foreign interests over the livelihoods of hardworking Americans, leaving a once-thriving industrial base in decline and countless families struggling to make ends meet. Exorbitant government spending, combined with crushing tax burdens, has devastated the middle class, pushing millions of hardworking citizens into poverty. The unconstitutional misuse of trillions in taxpayer dollars, funding fraud, abuse, and corruption has significantly weakened the nation. The United

States Constitution was designed to limit federal power and ensure a balance in governance. A bicameral Congress exists to represent the states (Senate) and the people (House of Representatives), with both chambers tasked with running government efficiently and responsibly. Federal law requires Congress to deliberate and approve the 12 appropriations of federal spending and produce a balanced budget annually. Yet Congress has failed to meet this obligation since 2005. Instead, year after year, they pass continuing resolutions, stuffed with unchecked spending, while repeatedly raising the debt ceiling. This negligence has added $27 trillion to the national debt across the terms of three presidents and six congresses. At the same time, over $3 trillion in wasteful spending occurs annually without accountability. The consequences are catastrophic: skyrocketing inflation, unsustainable debt, and an economy weakened by deliberate mismanagement. The cost of goods and services has risen dramatically, devastating American families. This reckless fiscal irresponsibility amounts to dereliction of duty, high crimes, and, ultimately, treason. Our government's failures, intentional or not, have weakened our nation, undermined its economy, and betrayed its people. These actions demand immediate intervention by "We the People" to restore accountability, constitutional governance, and the sovereignty of the United States.

Unconstitutional Expansion of Federal Government

The Constitution was explicitly designed to limit the powers of the federal government. The Tenth Amendment is clear: any powers not specifically granted to the federal government in the Constitution or prohibited to it by the states are reserved for the states or the people. Yet, over time, the federal government has usurped authority through a massive and unconstitutional expansion of its scope and influence. The federal government has intruded into areas where it has no constitutional authority, education, environmental protection, agriculture, housing, welfare, healthcare, land acquisition, and land management, among others. These overreaches exist solely to strip power from the states and the people, in direct violation of the Tenth Amendment. Every unconstitutional expansion of federal authority is a betrayal of the oath to support and defend the Constitution. Those responsible for these actions have abandoned their duty and undermined the principles of limited government upon which this nation was founded.

Corruption of the Judiciary

The judiciary, once intended to serve as a safeguard against tyranny and corruption, has been weaponized by entrenched bureaucrats and the deep state. The Department of Justice, FBI, numerous state attorneys' offices, and judicial benches across the nation have been compromised. From the orchestrated "Spy-gate" scandal and the Russia hoax to the corruption surrounding COVID-19 and the 2020 election, individuals in these institutions have committed high crimes against the nation. Judges, state attorneys, and law enforcement officials who should be the first line of defense against public corruption have instead violated their oaths, dishonoring themselves, their families, and their country. The treason committed by the highest offices in our government has been abetted by traitors within the judicial system. Their betrayal has undermined the rule of law, destroyed public trust, and facilitated a corrupt system that now threatens the very fabric of our republic.

Failure to Protect the Integrity of Our Elections

The two political parties have constructed an electoral system that systematically alienates candidates from outside their ranks. By doing so, they have corrupted our entire electoral process, including the Electoral College, to maintain their stranglehold on power.

Districts are notoriously gerrymandered to secure partisan strongholds, disenfranchising voters and undermining true representation. In 48 of the 50 states, the "winner-take-all" system of awarding electoral votes violates the very principles of the Constitution. This practice silences the voices of voters in dissenting districts, effectively stealing their representation and nullifying their votes. Moreover, the political parties have sold our government offices to the highest bidder through corporate donations and Super PACs, allowing outside money to influence elections at the expense of the constituencies being represented. Governments have a solemn responsibility to protect the integrity of elections, ensuring that every vote is counted and every voice heard. Instead, they have become the primary drivers of election fraud, voter irregularities, and unconstitutional practices designed to subvert the will of the people. This corruption undermines our democratic process, robs citizens of their voices, and violates the very principles upon which our republic was built. Election corruption is treason!

Collusion with Media

The government's collusion with a corrupt media establishment represents a direct attack on the principles of a free press, a cornerstone of our constitutional republic. The media, once tasked with holding power accountable, has become an instrument of disinformation and propaganda. Elite members of the government bureaucracy openly collaborate with media outlets to spread lies, sway public opinion, and manipulate election outcomes. Rather than reporting the truth or holding officials accountable, the media shields corrupt politicians, deceives the public, and fosters division and chaos among the citizenries. This collusion is not just a violation of journalistic integrity; it is an affront to the Constitution itself. The government's weaponization of the media has eroded trust, silenced dissent, and created an environment where tyranny can thrive.

Biological Warfare

In late 2019, the biological weapon COVID-19 was released on the world from the Wuhan Institute of Virology in China, with the United States as its primary target. Evidence suggests that factions within the American deep state, in collusion with foreign actors, orchestrated this act of biological warfare. Compromised U.S. political representatives with deep financial ties to Chinese corporations faced significant losses with the implementation of President Trump's China Trade Deal. The release of COVID-19 served multiple purposes for these bad actors: it undermined Trump's America First agenda, terminated the trade deal, and provided cover to steal the presidency and several congressional and senate seats through medical tyranny and election manipulation. This was not an isolated act; it was part of a coordinated plan to subvert the will of the American people. Under the guise of a global health emergency, the deep state leveraged fear and control to consolidate power and dismantle the progress of a movement that put the interests of the American people first. Further revelations of 46 additional Wuhan-style laboratories in Ukraine, funded by the U.S. Department of Defense, raise alarming questions about plans for future biological warfare. This evidence implicates the deep state in orchestrating not only past but potential future acts of genocide against its own citizens and the world. The release of COVID-19 was not merely a tragedy; it was treason. Those responsible for this biological warfare and its devastating consequences must be held accountable. They have violated the trust of the people and betrayed their country. Justice demands that they face the full weight of their crimes against humanity.

The Verdict

From the corruption of our elections to the perpetration of biological warfare, the actions of these entrenched political and bureaucratic elites represent a coordinated assault on the sovereignty of the United States and the rights of its citizens. Their crimes are treasonous, their betrayals profound, and their continued power untenable.

It is the duty of "We the People" to confront this corruption, demand justice, and restore the republic to its constitutional foundation. The time for action is now.

Reclaiming Our Government: The How and the Way Forward

Now that we understand what must be done and why it is necessary, it is time to address how we reclaim our government. This is a patriotic call to action, an organized, peaceful plan to unite veterans and patriots across the nation to reclaim our republic using the exact constitutional framework our Founding Fathers designed for dispelling tyranny.

"We the People" are the masters of our government. Every political office and every official, elected or appointed, serves at our discretion. Our Founding Fathers foresaw the dangers of political alliances and the tyranny such alliances could bring. In their wisdom, they created powerful constitutional remedies to ensure that the people could reclaim their government and stop tyranny in its tracks, without the need for violence. The Declaration of Independence is our unyielding guide. Its principles are eternal, declaring the inalienable rights endowed to us by our Creator and the civic duty of the people to defend and preserve these rights. The Declaration is not amendable; it is a foundational truth of our republic, forever engrained in its fabric.

"We hold these truths to be self-evident, that all men are created equal, that they are endowed by their Creator with certain unalienable rights, that among these are Life, Liberty, and the pursuit of Happiness. That to secure these rights, Governments are instituted amongst Men, deriving their just powers from the consent of the governed, that whenever any form of government becomes destructive of these ends, it is the Right of the People to alter or abolish it and to institute new Government, laying its foundation on such principles and organizing its powers in such form, as to them shall seem most likely to affect their Safety and Happiness."

This declaration speaks with undeniable authority: it is both the right and the duty of the people to preserve their unalienable rights and to reclaim their government when it becomes destructive to these ends. This is not an insurrection; we are not overthrowing our government. We the People are the government, and it is our civic duty to enforce Article VI, Clause III to remove all corrupt officials who have violated their sworn oaths to support and defend the Constitution. These blatant violations immediately disqualify the oath breakers from public service.

Phase One: Enforcing the Oaths Clause of the United States Constitution

The mission begins with the peaceful, swift, and constitutional enforcement of Article VI, Clause III, a solemn duty to uphold the very foundation of our republic. Our efforts will focus on electing constitutional sheriffs and commissioning constitutional courts within jurisdictions of constitutional counties, ensuring that justice is rooted in unwavering constitutional fidelity.

A constitutional judicial body will be established. Judges and prosecuting attorneys, empowered under their Article III authority, shall initiate the enforcement of Article VI with resolute determination. Writs of termination will be served to public servants charged with violating their oaths, oaths sworn to support, protect, and defend the Constitution of the United States. Evidence of high crimes and treason, upon consensus of constitutional sheriffs, shall be presented to the court. Warrants will be issued, and those who have engaged in corruption, committed high crimes, and betrayed the republic will face swift arrest, trial, and punishment to the fullest extent of the law.

Justice Shall be Served

Rebuilding Government: Restoring Constitutional Authority

All remaining officials who have not been complicit in corruption must renounce all political affiliations and swear an unbreakable allegiance to the institution of constitutional government. Only then will they be permitted to resume their positions. Ensuring Continuity of Government: Every vacancy created through termination or resignation shall be filled by steadfast patriots, individuals chosen for their unwavering commitment to the Constitution. These interim officials will take their oath with absolute resolve, pledging to restore and uphold a government that is truly: Of The People ~ By The People ~and For The People!

No compromise No exceptions The Republic shall stand!

The Role of "We The People" A Call to Action

The magnitude of this mission demands a force powerful enough to challenge and dismantle the entrenched corruption of a lawless government. The role of the people is clear:

We must rise once more, reviving "The Sons of Liberty" a formidable coalition of military veterans and patriots, one million strong. This is not just an initiative; it is a historic mandate to restore and safeguard the Republic. A Well-Regulated Militia being necessary for the security of a free state. A force of Justice with purpose and unity to protect the people's mission to institute constitutional government. It will stand as an unyielding shield against tyranny, ensuring that the will of the people prevails without compromise. The defense of liberty falls to those willing and able to bear the responsibility. We are the home of the brave, We are the Sons of Liberty of our time, This is our moment, The Republic Shall Rise Again.

Article V Convention of States, Restoring Constitutional Government

State legislatures shall invoke their authority to call a Convention of States for the re-establishment of constitutional governance. To ensure continuity of government, the people shall assemble an interim Congress. Its primary duty will be to immediately reinstate and uphold a true constitutional government, safeguarding the Republic and restoring power to We the People.

National State of Emergency & Martial Law

A national state of emergency and Martial law shall be declared to secure and stabilize the transition to new government. Martial law will remain in effect until all essential measures are fully implemented, operational, and ensuring the restoration of constitutional order. Once the reforms are complete, free and fair elections will be held, and the United States shall once again thrive as the constitutional republic it was always meant to be.

The Resolve to Act: A Call for Courage and Unity

This plan embodies the unshakable will of millions of hardworking, America-loving patriots. Though the challenge before us is great, we must recognize a fundamental truth: fear is the government's most powerful weapon against the people, a weapon it wields to silence, control, and oppress. The events of January 6th serve as a harsh reminder: when citizens assemble to even protest tyranny, the government responds with force and retaliation. But history has proven oppression cannot withstand the power of a unified people determined to defend liberty. The answer is unity and strength, a force so great that it cannot be ignored, silenced, or overpowered. With a clear strategy and unwavering resolve, good will prevail over evil. The Republic will be saved, and its future secured for generations to come.

The Call to Action: A Patriotic Mandate

If you've made it this far, it means The Revolution Blueprint has struck a chord with your love for this nation and your unwavering commitment to preserving our great constitutional republic. Now, the question is clear: How will you contribute to the fight for liberty?

Not everyone will take up an active role in the Sons of Liberty and that's okay. The coalition of patriots will be composed primarily of our nation's veterans, the men and women trained to defend this country and sworn to uphold the Constitution against all enemies, foreign and domestic. However, we cannot stand alone. our success depends on the support, strength, and dedication of everyday Americans. As patriots mobilize, logistical needs will arise, and it will be the countless patriots, men and women from all walks of life, who will rise to meet them, ensuring that this movement remains strong, effective, and unstoppable. We are in a fight for the future of our great country.

The First Act of Defiance: Severing Ties with a Corrupt System

Separation from affiliation is the most immediate and powerful step every patriotic American can take, an act of outright defiance, to immediately withdraw your political party affiliation from both the Democratic and Republican parties. This is not symbolic, it is essential. Neither party represents the people. Both are deeply corrupt, working to undermine our nation from within while allowing foreign adversaries to weaken us from afar. One cannot claim to stand for liberty and the constitution without first severing their ties to these domestic enemies.

This bold act of defiance carries profound consequences. It strips the two-party system of its greatest weapon, the illusion of public support. By renouncing our affiliations, we expose these parties as the criminal enterprises they are and reclaim our autonomy. Remaining tied to either party is no different than being complicit in their corruption, a fact most patriots already recognize. The charade ends with us. We withdraw our votes, reject their false choices, and refuse to participate in a system engineered to divide and control. Both parties thrive on the lie that one is simply the lesser of two evils, a trap that keeps us divided and powerless. It's time to break free and reject the game entirely.

The Second Act of Defiance: Rejecting Unconstitutional Mandates

Every unconstitutional mandate, restriction, or attempted reinstatement of COVID-style authoritarianism must be met with absolute defiance, without exception. We know that there is no constitutional authority behind such measures. There is no scientific justification for their enforcement. Health officials and executive authorities do not have unchecked power over public policy. In this republic, laws are made by legislatures, and even they cannot override the constitutional rights of the people. The response is simple: Defy all of it. Every single attempt. Reject them at every turn. At the same time, we must remain civil, disciplined, and unwavering in our commitment to law and order in all other respects. Allow patriots to organize, execute the mission, and restore the

Republic without interference. Defiance is not chaos. Defiance is the first step toward liberation.

The Path Forward: Unity, Strategy, and the Will of the People

The formation of patriots and the execution of Article VI enforcement will be followed by a meticulously crafted strategy, ensuring precision, efficiency, and readiness. Logistical frameworks and contingency plans have already been prepared. Once the largest citizen army in the world is assembled, a petition will be presented to the people, a declaration of intent to reclaim our government and institute constitutional government. The mission shall only proceed with unified consensus. A threshold of signatures will serve as an undeniable mandate from the people, ensuring that this movement represents the true voice of the nation.

A Call for Courage and Resolve

I ask just one more thing: Pray for our veterans and brave patriots, that they may rise with unshakable courage and an unyielding commitment to this cause. It will take just one-quarter of one percent of the citizenry to stand against tyranny and save the Republic. The stakes could not be higher. If we fail to act, the greatest experiment in liberty and self-governance will crumble, and our children will inherit a future of oppression we cannot yet fathom.

The patriot may risk everything when standing up to tyranny, but in our failure to act, we sentence our children to a future with a far worse fate. I will never look in the eyes of my son and admit I did nothing while his freedom was stolen. This is our moment and the time to act is now.

America's freedom was bought with courage, sacrifice, and iron resolve, and it now falls to us to defend it. We will not let the Republic fall while it is still ours to protect.

May God bless the patriots and, may God bless America.

RESTORING THE REPUBLIC: A CONSTITUTIONAL REBIRTH

The constitutional republic of the United States stands on the precipice of collapse. A shadow government operates behind the curtains of power, driven by corruption, collusion, and outright betrayal of the American people. We have witnessed treason at the highest levels, election manipulation, and medical tyranny imposed by those entrusted to uphold our freedoms. Top political leaders, military commanders, and federal and state judiciaries have engaged in blatant abuses of power, trampling on the very Constitution they swore an oath to defend. And what we see on the surface is only the tip of the iceberg, beneath it lies an entrenched system of deception, corruption, and lawlessness. The Democratic and Republican parties have hijacked the government, consolidating power for over a century. What has their uninterrupted rule given us? A century of failure, bad policies, unchecked incompetence, and an America in decline. Hyper-partisanship has rendered the government completely dysfunctional, incapable of meeting even the most basic needs of the nation. Laws are no longer executed faithfully and without prejudice, instead, the political elite have weaponized government agencies, law enforcement, and the judiciary against the American people. Public office is openly sold to the highest bidder, corrupt politicians, beholden to special interests, have abandoned their duty to serve the people. This political establishment has never represented the will of the people. They are the tyrannical government our Founding Fathers warned us about.

The Constitutional Remedy: Enforcing Article VI, Clause III

Fortunately, our Founders foresaw this moment and enshrined the constitutional solution in Article VI, Clause III. It is not just our right; it is our civic duty to intervene and restore constitutional governance. All individuals who have violated their sworn oath to uphold the Constitution must be removed from power and disqualified from public service. A new interim government must be sworn in, "of the people, by the people, and for the people."

The truth will be exposed. Once the people reclaim control of the government, the information that has been deliberately concealed will come to light, and those who have betrayed this nation will be held accountable. This is not a partisan battle; this is a fight for the survival of the Republic itself. The time for corruption is over. The time for constitutional restoration is now.

The Constitutional Pledge: A Commitment to Constitutional Restoration

With unwavering commitment, we take this Pledge, vowing to fully restore the United States as a true constitutional republic, one that is governed by the people, for the people, and never again vulnerable to tyranny. This pledge is not merely a statement of intent, it is a binding contract of duty and honor to ensure that no corrupt force shall ever again gain advantage over the American people.

Through Article V, Convention of States, the sovereign will of the people and the actions of a new Congress, we shall implement the seven acts of constitutional restoration outlined herein.

Furthermore, every individual sworn into office to replace those disqualified under Article VI, Clause III, shall be required to sign this pledge, a sacred oath to uphold and defend these principles. There will be no exceptions, no deviations, and no compromises, only absolute adherence to the Constitution and the will of the American people.

Together, we pledge to enact these seven acts, laying the foundation for a new order of governance that upholds the Constitution of the United States in its purest form, ensuring that America remains a free, sovereign, and unbreakable Republic for generations to come.

Act One: Secure the Border & Reform Immigration

A nation without secure borders is no nation at all. Unrestricted illegal immigration threatens national security, economic stability, and the rule of law. To restore sovereignty, we must immediately secure our borders, enforce strict immigration laws, and end the chaos that has undermined American communities for decades.

A. Build the Wall & Fortify Border Security

Construct a fortified border wall along all strategic entry points to prevent illegal crossings.

Implement advanced surveillance technology including drones, sensors, and AI-driven tracking systems. Expand and reinforce border patrol operations to maintain full coverage 24/7.

B. Deploy Military Forces to Secure the Border

Station the U.S. Army, Marines, and Coast Guard along the border, this is a national security imperative, not just an immigration issue. Authorize military forces to actively repel unauthorized crossings, dismantle smuggling networks, and prevent cartel infiltration.

Establish rapid response units to immediately intercept and process all illegal border activity.

C. Declare a National State of Emergency

All undocumented individuals who meet the established legal criteria must immediately apply for citizenship or face immediate deportation. Deploy the National Guard alongside federal and local law enforcement to enforce this mandate in every state.

Jail & deport all noncompliant individuals, there will be zero tolerance for illegal residency.

Execute mass deportations of all who fail to meet the strict legal standards for immigration, there will be no due process for non-citizens, and no exceptions to enforcement.

The Bottom line: America's Borders Will Be Defended. Sovereignty will be restored.

The invasion of illegal immigration will end. America's laws will be enforced, without exception.

Act Two: Taxation Reform, Restoring Fair & Constitutional Taxation

The current tax system is corrupt, unconstitutional, and weaponized against the American people. The IRS, with its 70,000+ pages of convoluted tax code, has become an instrument of government overreach and financial oppression. To restore economic freedom and constitutional governance, we must abolish the current tax system and replace it with a simple, transparent, and fair taxation model that funds government without overburdening the people.

A. Abolish the IRS & Eliminate the Corrupt Tax Code

Dismantle the IRS entirely, an agency that has been weaponized to target individuals, businesses, and political opponents. Eliminate the

70,000+ pages of complex, arbitrary, and unconstitutional tax laws that benefit the elite while punishing the working class.

End the income tax, corporate tax, estate tax, and capital gains tax, allowing Americans to keep what they earn and build generational wealth.

B. Constitutional Amendment: Repeal the 16th Amendment & Establish a Fair Tax System

Repeal the 16th Amendment, removing the federal government's power to impose an income tax and stripping it of any authority to seize wages. Replace all existing taxes with a single, simple national consumption tax. Implement a flat 10% National Sales Tax, ensuring everyone contributes equally, without loopholes or special exceptions.

C. Fair & Transparent Tax Distribution

Six percent (6%) of all sales tax revenue shall be allocated directly to state treasuries, ensuring that states retain financial independence. Four percent (4%) of all sales tax revenue shall be allocated directly to the U.S. Treasury, ensuring a limited but effective federal government.

The 10% tax rate shall be fixed, it cannot be increased or decreased, ensuring permanent protection against future government abuse.

The Bottom Line: Economic Freedom & Government Accountability

No more IRS. No more income tax. No more financial tyranny. A simple, fair, and transparent tax system that works for the people. A government funded by consumption, not by seizing the earnings of hardworking Americans. This is true taxation reform, restoring power to the people and the states, not the bureaucrats in Washington.

Act Three: Congressional Reforms

Restoring Integrity, Accountability, and Constitutional Governance

The United States Congress has become a breeding ground for corruption, self-interest, and dysfunction. Career politicians, special interest groups, and partisan elites have turned Congress into an institution of backroom deals, unchecked power, and financial exploitation, serving themselves rather than the people. This act restructures Congress, restores constitutional integrity, and ensures accountability at every level, making government serve the American people, not the ruling elite.

A. Repeal the 17th Amendment - Restore State Authority Over the Senate

State legislatures and governors shall regain control over Senate appointments, ensuring Senators serve their states, not federal interests. Senate appointments shall not exceed four-year terms, aligning with the tenure of their respective state governors.

This returns the Senate to its original constitutional purpose, representing the sovereignty of states, not political parties or special interests.

B. Term Limits - End the Era of Career Politicians

No Senator shall serve more than two terms (maximum of 8 years).

No House Representative shall serve more than three terms (maximum of six years).

No member of Congress shall serve beyond the age of 72.

Public service is a duty, not a lifelong career.

C. The People's Privilege Clause - Ban Political Alliances & Special Interests in Government

Elected officials, appointees, and government employees shall be strictly prohibited from political party affiliations, labor unions, or any organized alliances. Any official pledging loyalty to a party, caucus, or special interest group shall face immediate termination. Government exists to serve the people, not political machines.

D. Campaign Finance Reform - Ban Corporate & Special Interest Influence

Campaign funding shall be strictly limited, preventing financial corruption in elections.

All campaign funds must come from individual voters within the candidate's jurisdiction.

Contribution limits for Congressional candidates, state legislatures and all other local offices: Limited to 10 times the annual salary of the office sought. Gubernatorial candidates: Limited to 25 times the annual salary of the office sought. Presidential candidates: Limited to 100 times the annual salary of the office sought. Corporations, PACs, and all non-individual entities are prohibited from funding political campaigns. Elections must be decided by the people, not by corporate donors or special interests.

E. Budget Integrity Clause - No More Reckless Government Spending

All tax revenue shall be spent exclusively on American interests and citizens.

Foreign aid shall be limited to medical assistance and emergency food/water, and only through domestic agencies (e.g., Red Cross). No direct financial transfers to foreign governments.

Deficit spending is prohibited, government shall never spend beyond the revenue it generates.

Congress must pass a balanced budget annually before the start of the third fiscal quarter.

All spending bills must originate in the House and be subject to full transparency, line-item scrutiny, and independent voting.

F. The Government Efficiency Act - End Waste, Fraud, & Abuse

All government employees must meet high-performing standards or be replaced.

Excessive government spending beyond free-market pricing shall be illegal.

Contract procurement shall operate on a blind, low-bid system, eliminating corruption and favoritism.

G. The Government Accountability Act - Demand 100% Truth in Government

All government agencies shall be held to a strict standard of absolute transparency.

No official may mislead, distort, or misrepresent facts to the American people.

Violators shall face immediate removal from office or employment.

H. The Legislative Integrity Clause - End Political Manipulation in Lawmaking

All bills must be singular in issue, no more multi-topic bills stuffed with hidden policies.

All bills must be fewer than 100 pages, no more unreadable legal jargon to conceal corruption.

All members of Congress must read the full bill before voting. Each bill must stand on its own merit, no more backroom deals or political bargaining. Congress shall be prohibited from consulting with or accepting influence from lobbyists.

I. The Election Integrity Clause - Secure and Fair Elections

All elections shall have a two-stage process: A primary election followed by a general election between the top two candidates. Gubernatorial and Presidential elections shall be determined by individual congressional districts, with electoral votes awarded per district won, ensuring every district has a voice in executive elections.

Voting regulations:

All votes must be cast in person on Election Day, using paper ballots. Voters must present state-issued ID and voter registration. Mail-in ballots are restricted to military and government personnel overseas, and disabled citizens. Mail-in ballots must be requested, postmarked 48 hours before Election Day, and remain sealed until counting begins. Electronic voting systems are strictly prohibited, paper ballots ensure a transparent, tamper-proof election.

J. The Legislative Powers Clause, Restore State & Federal Authority, End Bureaucratic Overreach

Lawmaking powers shall reside solely with elected legislatures at the state and federal levels.

No federal agency shall have the power to create, mandate, or enforce regulations outside legislative authority. All criminal prosecutions shall be handled by state governments in the state and jurisdiction where the crime has been committed, in adherence to the constitution.

K. The Right to Learn Clause - Protect Education from Political Indoctrination

All public and private schools must focus on core subjects: Civics, American history, mathematics, science, and financial literacy.

Anti-American or anti-constitutional teachings shall be prohibited.

Any individual or institution engaging in anti-America, anti-constitution treasonous indoctrination shall face loss of citizenship and permanent deportation.

L. The Equal Education Clause - Restore Standardized, Accountable Education

Each state shall have a single education department with one unified curriculum.

All public schools shall follow a uniform standard, ensuring equal education for all students.

School boards and teachers' unions shall be prohibited and permanently abolished.

M. The Anti-Grooming Act - Protect Children from Exploitation & Political Agendas

Any form of sexual education in K-12 schools is strictly prohibited.

Curriculum shall focus on academics, not ideological or sexual content.

The role of sex education belongs to parents, no exceptions.

Restoring a Government That Serves the People

Congress will be stripped of corruption and returned to its constitutional function.

Laws will be simple, transparent, and accountable. Elections will be secure, fair, and free from special interest influence. Education will be restored to its true purpose of teaching children the skills necessary to become productive adult members of society No more unchecked spending, no more bureaucratic overreach, no more government lies. This is a government for the people, not for career politicians, corporate elites, or corrupt institutions.

Act Four: Judicial and Policing Reform

Restoring Justice, Accountability, and Constitutional Integrity

The judicial system and law enforcement institutions have been corrupted by political influence, bureaucratic overreach, and a blatant disregard for the citizen's constitutional rights. Justice is no longer blind, impartial, or equally applied, instead, it has become a weapon wielded by the powerful against the people. This sweeping reform will restore fairness, accountability, and the rule of law, ensuring that every citizen is truly equal under the law and that law enforcement serves and protects, rather than controls and oppresses.

A. The Presumption of Innocence Clause - No Convictions Without Jury Trial

Abolish plea agreements, no person shall be convicted or punished without a trial.

Innocent until proven guilty, the burden of proof shall always rest with the prosecution.

No court shall deny a defendant their right to present evidence in their defense, regardless of judicial discretion or opinion. Courts shall be duty-bound to protect citizens from unfair prosecution, the justice system shall serve the people, not persecute them.

B. The Compliance Clause - Zero Tolerance for Constitutional Violations

No public official or government employee shall retain their position after violating their constitutional oath. Judges who infringe upon constitutional rights shall be immediately disqualified from office. All members of the judiciary must prioritize the constitutional rights of citizens above all else.

C. The Accountability Clause - No Immunity for Public Officials

Public officials are an extension of government and shall not be protected by the 5th Amendment in matters related to their official duties. This clause applies retroactively and prospectively, ensuring that all past, present, and future officials are held accountable. Public service must come with full transparency and accountability, no official shall hide behind legal loopholes.

D. The Anti-Immunity Clause - Government Shall Not Protect Itself from Consequences

No law shall shield government agencies, officials, or corporations from liability for actions that harm citizens. Due process cannot be selectively applied, if the government acts unlawfully, it must be held accountable. No entity shall be above the law, and no bureaucratic shields shall exist to protect those who violate the rights of the people.

E. The People's Judiciary Clause - Justice Must Be Fair, Accessible, and Equal for All

The judiciary shall be simplified and fully accessible to all citizens, free from bureaucratic obstruction. Equal representation shall be guaranteed for all defendants and plaintiffs, regardless of financial status. The government is prohibited from restricting a citizen's right to legal representation in any capacity. All legal representation shall be provided through a state or federal judiciary system, ensuring fairness in all cases. Private attorneys shall be prohibited from practicing law in criminal, tort, and family law cases, all licensed attorneys must be employed or contracted by the judiciary. Attorneys shall be assigned to cases blindly and without prejudice, preventing judicial corruption and favoritism.

Citizens may request a change of attorney at their discretion to ensure competent representation.

F. The Father's Rights Clause - Equal Rights for Parents in Family Law

Fathers shall have equal guardianship and custodial rights as mothers.

No government shall forcibly seize or redistribute parental assets.

Each parent shall provide housing, clothing, and food for their children while in their custody.

Parental financial responsibility shall be equally shared, with no consideration of income or assets. State Government assistance programs shall not discriminate against married couples, ensuring equal support for all families in need.

G. The Law Enforcement Reciprocity Clause - Strengthening Sheriff's Departments as Constitutional Defenders

Sheriff's departments shall be the primary law enforcement agencies of the land, operating independently of any political influence. Sheriffs shall uphold the Constitution above all else and execute the laws of their state and jurisdiction faithfully. Sheriffs shall have full prosecutorial discretion within their jurisdiction, prosecutors must act on cases recommended for prosecution by the sheriff's office. Sheriffs shall have the authority to arrest both private citizens and public officials within their jurisdiction. All sheriff and deputy sheriff positions shall be elected by the people. Sheriffs shall have full power to deputize deputies to meet the policing demands within their jurisdictions. State and local governments shall be required to fully fund the sheriff's departments, ensuring adequate resources for public safety. Law enforcement personnel shall be held to the highest physical and intellectual standards, ensuring only the most capable individuals serve.

All sheriff's deputies shall undergo continuous tactical and conflict resolution training and meet physical fitness standards equivalent to the United States Marine Corps.

The Bottom Line: Restoring Justice and Law Enforcement to Serve the People

The presumption of innocence will be absolute.

The judiciary shall be fully accessible, fair, and free of corruption.

Public officials will be held accountable for their actions, with no immunity.

Parents will be given equal rights in raising their children.

Sheriff's departments will be the guardians of constitutional law, fully independent from political influence. Law enforcement will be highly trained, highly capable, and held to the highest standards. This reform puts power back where it belongs, with the people. Justice shall no longer be a tool of oppression but a true safeguard of liberty.

Act Five: Restoring State Sovereignty & Nullification

For far too long, the federal government has overstepped its constitutional boundaries, expanding into areas where it was never intended to have authority. This unchecked federal overreach has stripped the states of their sovereignty, consolidating power in Washington D.C. and rendering state governments subservient rather than independent. This act restores the rightful balance of power, reigns in the federal government, and reaffirms the sovereignty of the states as independent republics united under a common cause, liberty.

A. Enforce the Tenth Amendment - Nullify All Unconstitutional Federal Agencies

Dismantle all federal agencies and programs that exceed the constitutional powers enumerated to the federal government. The U.S. Constitution is precise and specific in delegation of powers to the federal government, and any overreach beyond those powers must be nullified.

The federal government exists solely to ensure national security, foreign diplomacy, and to provide a platform for state cooperation. It was never meant to dictate state governance.

The states are sovereign entities, independent republics within a union, not subordinate to a central authority. The American people will reclaim the limited federal government intended by the Founding Fathers, ensuring that state authority is fully restored, and that Washington is returned to its constitutional role, and nothing more.

B. The Single Layer of Government Clause - Ending Federal Redundancy & Overreach

A constitutional amendment shall establish that only one layer of government shall exist in any area where government is necessary. If governance belongs at the state level, the federal government shall be prohibited from interfering. Federal authority shall not extend into areas where states must operate independently to maintain their sovereignty. No more redundant federal bureaucracy. No more federal overreach into state affairs. No more centralized control undermining the authority of the states.

This is a return to the true American model, where the federal government is limited, restrained, and focused on national security, while state governments retain their rightful autonomy to govern their own affairs.

The Bottom Line: Restoring True Federalism. State sovereignty will be fully reinstated.

The federal government will be strictly limited to its constitutional powers.

All unconstitutional federal agencies will be dismantled.

Each state will govern itself without interference from Washington D.C.

The era of federal tyranny ends here, power will be returned to the states and the people, where it rightfully belongs.

Act Six: Media & Big Tech Reforms - Restoring Truth, Integrity, and Free Speech

The mainstream media and big tech companies have corrupted public discourse, manipulated elections, and actively colluded with government to suppress free speech, silence dissent, and spread propaganda. The corporate-controlled information industry no longer serves as a watchdog for the people, it has become a weapon of deception, manipulation, and tyranny.

This act restores journalistic integrity, protects the First Amendment, and dismantles the corrupt media-industrial complex that has undermined democracy and eroded trust in public discourse.

A. The Truth in Media Act - Holding Journalists Accountable

Media outlets shall be strictly prohibited from lying, misleading, or spreading disinformation to the public. Journalists shall be banned by law from colluding with government officials, political candidates, their campaigns, or any affiliated entities. Any journalist found guilty of knowingly misrepresenting facts, colluding with politicians, or spreading disinformation shall face permanent revocation of their journalism license. The media shall return to its rightful role, reporting facts, not manufacturing narratives. Journalistic ethics and accountability shall be mandatory, not optional.

B. The Communications Integrity Act - Ending Big Tech Censorship

Social media platforms, search engines, and technology providers shall be strictly prohibited from censoring content or suppressing free speech.

All published content shall be recognized as protected speech under the First Amendment.

Any platform or tech company engaging in censorship shall face an immediate and permanent suspension of its FCC license. Violators shall be subject to severe criminal penalties, including asset forfeiture and prosecution for constitutional violations.

There is ZERO TOLERANCE for any entity that attempts to control public discourse.

Big Tech will no longer decide what Americans can or cannot say.

Free speech will be protected in all digital and media spaces, no exceptions.

C. Disband and Prosecute Corrupt Media & Tech Entities

Any media or tech company found guilty of colluding with government officials to suppress truth, spread propaganda, or interfere with elections shall be permanently disbanded.

Executives, journalists, and employees involved in these crimes shall face arrest and prosecution. All individuals who participated in aiding or abetting COVID-era tyranny shall be arrested and prosecuted for crimes against the United States.

The media-industrial complex will be dismantled.

No entity shall hold the power to manipulate the people ever again.

The Bottom Line: A Free and Honest Information Industry

Journalistic integrity will be legally enforced.

Big Tech censorship will be permanently outlawed.

Media collusion and propaganda will result in swift justice.

The First Amendment will be fully restored and fiercely protected.

The era of lies, suppression, and state-controlled narratives is over.

Truth will reign. Free speech will be absolute. The people will decide the future of this nation, not corporate elites.

Act Seven: Commissioning a National Association of Sheriffs as a Permanent Government Policing Authority

For far too long, government agencies have been weaponized against the people, serving political elites instead of upholding justice and defending constitutional rights. The FBI and other federal policing bodies have engaged in unchecked corruption, political persecution, and violations of civil liberties, all while operating without meaningful oversight. This act establishes the National Association of Sheriffs as the ultimate enforcement authority of the Republic, ensuring that government remains accountable to the people and never again becomes a tool of tyranny.

A. The Republic Defense Clause - Establishing a Citizen-Led National Association of Sheriffs

The National Association of Sheriffs (NAS) shall be commissioned as a permanent civil defense force. The NAS shall be proportionally distributed among the states based on state population, ensuring every state has an adequate force for civic defense, investigation, and oversight. The NAS shall be fully funded as a civil defense priority, with each state's budget allocating funds according to its sheriff membership. The NAS shall determine its own budget and govern itself independently, free from political interference. A government of the people, by the people, and for the people shall be policed by direct representatives of the people. This ensures that no centralized government force can oppress the people, override state sovereignty, or abuse its power without facing immediate accountability.

B. The Tyranny Defense Clause - National Association of Sheriffs Oversight & Reform of Federal Investigations. The NAS shall assume full control over the Federal Bureau of Investigations and all of its facilities, equipment, and operations. The FBI, as it currently stands, shall be disbanded, and all corrupt or non-compliant personnel shall be purged immediately. The NAS shall redefine the mission of federal investigations, prioritizing the investigation of government officials and agencies throughout all governments for crimes committed against the Constitution and the people. The NAS shall have full oversight and arresting powers over ALL elected and non-elected personnel serving in government at federal, state, and local levels.

Through a democratic process, all sheriffs throughout the United States shall vote to form the National Association of Sheriffs High Council, which shall be entrusted with the authority to appoint and expel leadership responsible for investigations of public officials.

This ensures that no agency will ever again be corrupted by bureaucracy, weaponized against the people's interests, or placed above the law.

Never again will a government agency operate outside the reach of the citizens.

Never again will political elites escape accountability.

Never again will the people be left defenseless against government overreach.

The Bottom Line: The People Will Police Their Own Government

The National Association of Sheriffs will serve as the ultimate check on government power.

The people, not politicians, will control government investigations and law enforcement through the sheriffs they elect to serve them. Sheriffs from across the nation will form the NAS High Council, ensuring that leadership is chosen by those directly accountable to the people, not by political elites or bureaucrats. Through this structure, government agencies will be purged of corruption and held to the highest standards of constitutional accountability.

No government official, elected or unelected, will be immune from prosecution.

No agency will ever again be weaponized against the citizens it is sworn to protect.

This act ensures that power remains exactly where it belongs: with the people.

Government corruption will be exposed, investigated, and punished swiftly.

Tyranny will never again take root in America.

The Constitutional Pledge Summary:

Act One - Securing the Border & Restoring Sovereignty

Border security is not optional, it is a matter of our nation's survival. A nation without secure borders ceases to be a nation. The first constitutional responsibility of the federal government is to protect the sovereignty and security of the United States by preventing invasion and maintaining order. This is an elementary principle practiced by every sovereign nation worldwide. For decades, corrupt politicians from both parties have deliberately failed to secure our borders, leading to unchecked illegal immigration, cartel violence, human trafficking, and the flood of deadly narcotics into our communities. The current invasion of millions of illegal migrants has placed an unbearable strain on law enforcement and public services throughout the nation. This failure is no longer just a civic issue, it is a national security crisis.

To reclaim our sovereignty, restore order, and end the decades-long invasion, we must take decisive action:

Action One: Deploy the Military to Secure the Border & Dismantle the Cartels

The U.S. Army, Marines, and Coast Guard shall be deployed to the southern border. All illegal crossings will be intercepted, and all unauthorized entrants will be immediately detained or turned back. Military forces should be dispatched into Mexico to target and eliminate cartel operations, ending the drug and human trafficking networks that have devastated communities for decades. Cartel activity at the border directly fuels crime across the United States. By confronting the cartels head-on, we will save over 300,000 American lives per year. No more open borders. No more cartel rule in border communities. No more lawlessness.

Action Two: Build the Wall & Fortify Border Infrastructure

Construct the border wall as originally promised by President Donald J. Trump.

Fortify high-risk entry points with state-of-the-art surveillance, security checkpoints, and rapid-response military units. Ensure no gaps, no weak spots, and no easy pathways for illegal crossings. Physical barriers combined with military enforcement will make illegal entry near impossible.

Action Three: Execute a National Emergency Declaration & Mass Deportation Effort

All undocumented individuals inside the U.S. will be required to register and apply for citizenship within 90 days of policy implementation. There will be ZERO exceptions, failure to comply will result in immediate imprisonment, and permanent deportation after time served.

All undocumented individuals must prove they have resided in the U.S. for over five years (prior to January 2020) to be eligible for consideration. Any individual who does not meet these criteria will face immediate deportation. Criminal aliens, high-risk individuals, and those engaged in illicit activity will be deported immediately. Lower-risk individuals will be given a limited grace period for voluntary self-deportation, failure to comply will result in arrest, imprisonment, and permanent expulsion.

Action Four: Migrant Assimilation & Citizenship Reform

Of the estimated 20 million undocumented individuals residing in the U.S. for over five years, only those who meet current immigration standards will be allowed to apply for citizenship.

Applicants must: Demonstrate good moral character. Pass an English language proficiency test.

Pass a U.S. citizenship test. Prove financial self-sufficiency and ability to contribute to society.

Pledge full allegiance to the United States of America. Federal employees reassigned from terminated agencies could be mobilized to process applications efficiently. This is not amnesty, this is controlled and enforced immigration reform. No more illegal status, either they register, assimilate, and contribute, or they are deported.

Why This Plan is Necessary & Justified

For decades, weak leadership and corrupt politicians have failed to enforce immigration laws. The American people trusted the government to secure the border, but it has willfully neglected its duties. Now, we must take extraordinary action to correct this failure. We cannot deport 20 million people overnight, but we CAN force every undocumented individual to come out of the shadows, register, and be fully accounted for. We will finally separate those who contribute to society from those who are a threat to it. We will eliminate the criminal elements that have been hiding among the masses. With the abolishment of the IRS and the termination of unconstitutional government programs, the U.S. economy will boom, creating millions of new jobs. Those who legitimately earn their citizenship will contribute to this prosperity, while those who violate our laws will be permanently expelled. The Hispanic and immigrant communities in America include many hardworking, family-oriented, God-fearing individuals who share our American values. A path to citizenship that is lawful, fair, and accountable is the best alternative for the nation. In our new republic, no one will live in the shadows, and all will pay their fair share, be represented, and be treated equally under the law.

National Security Crisis: The Enemy is Inside the Gates

The recent failures of the Obama controlled Biden administration, has resulted in millions of fighting-age males from foreign nations illegally entering the U.S. This is not just a border issue; This is an active invasion. We do not know who these individuals are. We do not know their intentions. We do not know how many are aligned with foreign adversaries or terrorist organizations. The National Guard, in conjunction with ICE, will be tasked with locating and removing all high-risk individuals from our interior. This is no longer a political issue; this is a matter of national defense. The enemy is already inside our borders, and we will remove them by force if necessary.

The Bottom Line: America's Borders Will Be Defended. Period.

Illegal immigration will be ended permanently.

The military will enforce border security and eliminate cartel operations.

All illegal entrants will be forced to register, assimilate, or leave.

The wall will be built, fortified, and made impenetrable.

Criminal aliens and high-risk individuals will be purged from the nation.

The security of our nation and its sovereignty will never again be compromised.

This is how we secure America's future. This is how we reclaim our sovereignty. This is how we protect our people. No more excuses. No more delays. No more compromises.

Act Two - Abolishing the IRS & Restoring Economic Freedom

The abolition of the IRS and the elimination of unconstitutional taxation is essential to restoring individual liberty and economic prosperity in the United States. The current tax system is a mechanism of control, oppression, and wealth redistribution, designed to enrich the political elite while enslaving hardworking Americans. For too long, the government has exploited its power to tax as a weapon against the people, stripping us of our earnings at every turn:

Taxed on our income

Taxed on our purchases

Taxed on our homes and property

Taxed on license, energy, fuel, capital gains, inheritance, and even death

The layers of taxation imposed on Americans are in direct violation of our unalienable right to liberty and stand in direct opposition to the founding principles of this nation. The 16th Amendment was never intended to authorize unlimited taxation, yet corruption in government has transformed it into a system of wealth confiscation and government overreach.

This act restores economic freedom by eliminating the IRS, ending all forms of income taxation, and replacing the corrupt system with a simple, transparent, and fair tax model that serves the people, not the Central Bank!

Action One: Abolish the IRS & Eliminate the Corrupt Tax Code

The IRS will be permanently dismantled, and its 70,000+ pages of corrupt tax code will be eliminated in their entirety. All income taxes, corporate taxes, estate taxes, capital gains taxes, and property taxes will be abolished. No longer will the federal government have the power to seize a portion of a citizen's labor. The government's ability to manipulate markets, pick winners and losers, and redistribute wealth through taxation will end. Americans will no longer be threatened with audits, penalties, or imprisonment for failing to pay an unconstitutional tax.

No more IRS. No more weaponized taxation. No more government theft.

Action Two: Repeal the 16th Amendment & End the Government's Power to Tax Income

The 16th Amendment does not grant Congress the power to enforce its provisions, therefore, it is not binding law. Article 1, Section 8 of the Constitution, enumerates power to lay duties and collect taxes for specific spending purposes, pay the national debts, the common defense and general welfare of the United States. Congress has violated this power by using taxpayer money to fund foreign governments, facilitate illegal immigration, and wage wars that do not serve our national security interests. By aiding and abetting the invasion of our borders with tax-payer dollars, Congress is actively committing treason. The people must intervene and reclaim their economic liberty by repealing the 16th Amendment and ending unconstitutional taxation forever.

Action Three: Implement a National Consumption Tax, The Only Fair & Constitutional Tax System. A simple 10% national sales tax will be applied to all goods and services, ensuring that all revenue is generated fairly, transparently, and in alignment with free-market principles.

Six percent (6%) of all revenue will go directly to state governments. Four percent (4%) will fund the federal government, ensuring a strictly limited national budget. No additional taxes will be permitted at any level of government, ending property taxes, income taxes, excise taxes, and all forms of wealth confiscation. Tax revenue will be based purely on consumption, meaning those who spend more pay more, while those who spend less pay less. No more tax loopholes. No more corporate favoritism. No more government picking winners and losers. Every American, every business, and every industry will pay their fair share based solely on what they consume.

Funding Government - A national consumption tax generates revenue by taxing voluntary economic activity, what people and businesses choose to spend, not what they earn or own. This method ties government funding directly to the strength and participation of the free market, not to forced confiscation through income or property taxes. Because money is never static, but constantly moving through the economy, the same dollar is spent, earned, and re-spent many times over. This constant rate of exchange, known as the velocity of money, ensures that a simple 10% consumption tax captures revenue multiple times from the same dollar. For example, when a dollar is taxed at 10% each time it is spent, and that dollar changes hands ten times, it effectively generates a total of 100% in tax revenue without ever overburdening any single transaction or individual. This natural multiplying effect provides a steady, reliable, and transparent funding stream that grows with economic activity without the need for high tax rates, wealth confiscation, or government manipulation. Under this system, 6% of all revenue collected will be directed to state governments, and 4% will fund the federal government. No other taxes will be permitted at any level, ending income taxes, property taxes, excise taxes, and all forms of forced wealth extraction.

Key principles to understand about the economic theory behind a 10% consumption tax model

Total U.S. Economy 2024 (GDP)- Roughly $28 trillion. GDP = total economic output, but GDP is only a measure of final goods and services, it does not count all intermediate transactions or financial flows that happen behind the scenes. With this plan, everything is taxed at the point of transaction:

1. Goods (retail, wholesale, imports)
2. Services (labor, professional services, utilities, insurance)
3. Real Estate (buying and selling property)
4. Energy (electric, gas, water bills)
5. Financial Transactions (everything from a haircut, to meals, to an oil change)

This massively increases the taxable base far beyond just consumer spending.

This theory bases the revenue estimate on the full-spectrum 10% tax across all economic transactions. Financial Transactions and Business Activity Multiplier, (Business-to-business commerce) is also massive. Financial transactions (stocks, insurance, real estate) add many trillions more. Energy, phone, utilities, services are constant recurring transactions.

Studies estimate that the total financial transactional volume in the U.S. is 20 to 50 times larger than GDP when you count all exchanges (source: Bank of International Settlements estimates on transactional flows).

Conservative Estimate: Assume total taxable economic activity = 5x GDP (very conservative).

$28 trillion × 5 = $140 trillion taxable base annually.

Applying 10% consumption tax: $140 trillion x 10% = $14 trillion

By Comparison:

The current U.S. Tax Revenue from all sources = > $5 trillion

The State and Local tax revenue from all sources = < $3 trillion

Total spending, Federal, State and Local Government = $12 trillion

Proposed National Consumption Tax estimate = $14 trillion

A Consumption Tax Will Unleash the Greatest Economic Boom in History. The government and mainstream media have conditioned Americans to believe that income tax is the only viable way to fund government operations, this is a lie. The truth is that a consumption-based tax system will generate substantial surplus revenue to sustain a constitutional government while dismantling the corrupt tax structure, ending economic oppression.

Some critical insights into the economic dynamics of a 10% consumption-based tax system.

The 10% national consumption tax is not merely a reform; it is a total economic revolution. It tears down the corrupt structure of confiscating income, property, and investment and replaces it with a voluntary, transparent model that empowers the people and shackles government expansion. Under this system, every financial transaction in America; goods, services, labor, utilities, real estate, imports, and investments, would be taxed at one simple, fair rate. With the U.S. economy producing over $28 trillion GDP annually, and the full velocity of money multiplying that figure many times over, this model would conservatively generate $14 trillion or more in revenue every year, far surpassing the bloated collections of today's IRS-driven regime. No more punishments for success. No more government manipulation through complex tax codes. No more weaponized bureaucracy crushing prosperity. Transitioning to this model would immediately unleash historic economic growth. The American workforce would save an estimated $3.2 trillion annually in federal and state taxes, while businesses would save approximately $2.5 trillion each year. On top of that, it would eliminate over 6.5 billion wasted hours and $413 billion currently spent just complying with today's complex tax regulations. These savings would flood back into the economy, fueling investment, expansion, and wealth creation. Consumer purchasing power would surge by trillions of dollars, igniting record-setting economic expansion. The elimination of corporate tax and compliance burdens would lead to massive job creation, drastically improving job availability and driving substantial wage increases across all sectors. America would become the most attractive economy in the world, pulling in unprecedented levels of investment and innovation. Government waste, fraud, and abuse would be largely eradicated, ensuring that tax revenue is used strictly for essential public services. With no income tax, every American would immediately take home 100% of their earnings, allowing families to build generational wealth, invest freely, and secure their future.

With no property tax, Americans would truly own their homes free from perpetual government claims. With no corporate tax, businesses would reinvest in higher wages, expansion, and entrepreneurship sparking a golden age of American prosperity. This is not just theory. This is the path to the greatest economic renaissance in world history. Power over taxation and therefore power over government returns to where it has always belonged: We the People.

Debunking the Myths: The Consumption Tax is the Ultimate Equalizer

In simple terms, it works like this: If I spend $1,000, I pay $100 in tax, clear, fair, and straightforward. Under the current system, if I earn $1,000, the government takes $350 off the top and then taxes me again every time I spend, then taxes me on my home, taxes my investments, and piles on countless other fees and costs. One system punishes success and drains freedom. The other lets you keep what you earn and only pay when you choose to spend. Opponents claim that a consumption tax disproportionately affects the poor. This is mathematically false. Lower-income individuals who spend less will naturally pay less in taxes, while those who spend more will pay more. If someone spends $200 per week on essentials, they contribute just $20 in tax, a fair and manageable share tied directly to their voluntary participation in the economy. Meanwhile, a wealthier individual spending $2,000 per week would contribute $200 in tax, ten times more, naturally carrying a proportionally greater share without government force or coercion. The consumption tax model also ensures that no one escapes paying their fair share. Illegal workers, drug dealers, and all who previously operated under the table will be taxed equally every time they spend a dollar. Every dollar spent generates tax revenue again and again as it moves through the economy, fueling an endless cycle of growth, innovation, and prosperity. The poor will not be taxed into poverty.

The rich will no longer exploit tax loopholes. Illegal income will no longer escape taxation.

Every American will contribute based on what they choose to consume, no more, no less.

This is real fairness. This is real freedom.

The Bottom Line: The Era of Government Theft Ends Here

The IRS will be permanently abolished. The 16th Amendment will be repealed, and income tax will be forever banned. A simple, fair, and transparent consumption tax will replace the corrupt system. The American people will take home 100% of their earnings, free from government confiscation. Our economy will explode with historic growth, job creation, and prosperity.

The government will be forced to operate within its constitutional limits, no more reckless spending, no more financial oppression. This act doesn't just reform the tax system, it completely destroys the corrupt foundation that has enslaved generations of Americans to government control. This is true economic freedom. No more income tax. No more job tax. No more capital gains tax. No more estate tax. No more excise tax. Freedom will reign from this point forward! The greatest lie the government ever sold was that it needs YOUR money to survive. The truth is America has been held hostage by a system designed to keep YOU as slaves working for them. When the time for taxation tyranny ends, the time for economic liberation begins.

Act Three - Reforming Congress & Restoring Legislative Integrity

For over a century, Congress has been controlled by two political parties that have consolidated power, rigged the system in their favor, and abandoned their duty to the people and the states. This alliance of political elites has created a corrupt, unaccountable, and tyrannical legislative branch that no longer serves its intended constitutional purpose. The Founding Fathers warned against the dangers of party-controlled government and designed a system where the people, the states, and the executive branch each had a coequal voice in federal governance. Through constitutional amendments, fraudulent policies, and deliberate power grabs, Congress has stripped the states of their representation, ignored the will of the people, and placed partisan loyalty above their oath of office. This act restores Congress to its proper constitutional function, ensuring that lawmakers answer only to the people and the states, not political parties, special interests, or corporate donors.

Action One: Repeal the 17th Amendment - Restore the States' Power Over the Senate

The power to appoint U.S. Senators shall return to state legislatures and their governors.

The Senate was never meant to represent the people, it was designed to represent state sovereignty. Since the 17th Amendment, senators have abandoned their duty to the states, leaving state governments voiceless in federal legislation. Repealing the 17th Amendment would restore the original constitutional balance of power by making U.S. Senators accountable to their state governments rather than to political parties, corporations, or national special interests. This change would reestablish state sovereignty within the federal system, ensuring that federal legislation reflects the needs and rights of individual states, not just the ambitions of centralized power in Washington, D.C.

Action Two: Impose Congressional Term Limits & End Career Politicians

Senators shall be limited to two terms (8 years). House Representatives shall be limited to three terms (6 years). No member of Congress shall serve beyond the age of 72. Congressional service shall be a civic duty, not a lifelong career. No pensions, lifetime benefits, or post-office compensation, public service is not a get-rich scheme. Imposing term limits and ending lifetime congress-ional careers would break the cycle of corruption, entrenchment, and self-serving governance. It would restore the idea of public service as a temporary civic duty, not a path to personal enrichment. By rotating new leaders through Congress and eliminating lifetime benefits, the system would stay more accountable, connected to the people, and resistant to special interests and political machines. The era of career politicians ends with this amendment.

Action Three: The People's Privilege Clause - Ban Political Party Affiliation in Government

Elected officials are there to serve the people, not political parties. Any elected or appointed official who pledges allegiance to a political party over their constituents shall be immediately removed from office. Partisan voting blocks and political alliances that prevent independent deliberation will be banned. Government officials will be loyal to their oath, their office, and the Constitution, not a political party. Banning political party affiliation within government would dismantle partisan loyalty that undermines independent judgment and constitutional duty. Officials would be accountable solely to their constituents, their oath, and the Constitution, restoring integrity, reducing corruption, and ensuring that laws are made based on principle, not political party agendas.

Action Four: Campaign Finance Reform - Eliminate Corporate & Special Interest Influence

Only registered voters within a district or state may contribute to a candidate's campaign.

Corporations, super PACs, and outside organizations shall be strictly prohibited from financing political campaigns. Strict campaign spending limits shall be set, preventing billion-dollar election cycles. Elections will be decided by the people, not by corporate money or foreign influence. Eliminating corporate, PAC, and special interest funding from elections would return political power to the voters, ensuring that elections are decided by the people, not by billion-dollar influence campaigns. This reform would level the playing field, reduce corruption, and restore the integrity of the democratic process by preventing outside money and foreign interests from controlling American elections.

Action Five: The Budget Integrity Clause - End Reckless Government Spending

The federal budget shall be strictly limited to constitutional powers and responsibilities. Congress shall pass a balanced budget every year, deficit spending shall be permanently prohibited. All foreign aid shall be restricted to humanitarian assistance only, no direct financial transfers to foreign governments. Massive spending bills filled with pork, waste, and fraud shall be outlawed. No more endless debt. No more reckless spending. No more money laundering through foreign aid. Strictly limiting the federal budget to constitutional responsibilities and banning deficit spending would end the cycle of reckless debt accumulation and financial corruption. By requiring a balanced budget and eliminating wasteful foreign aid and pork-barrel spending, this reform would restore fiscal discipline, protect future generations from unsustainable debt, and ensure that taxpayer dollars are used solely for legitimate public purposes.

Action Six: The Government Efficiency Act - Eliminate Waste, Fraud, & Bureaucracy

The federal government shall adopt private-sector efficiency standards to eliminate unnecessary spending. All government contracts shall be awarded based on competitive, blind bidding, no more political favoritism. Government employees shall meet strict performance standards, no more unaccountable bureaucrats collecting paychecks for doing nothing.

Taxpayer dollars will be used efficiently, or not at all. Adopting private-sector efficiency standards and enforcing competitive, merit-based government operations would slash waste, fraud, and bureaucratic corruption. By holding government employees and contractors accountable to strict performance and bidding standards, this reform would ensure that taxpayer dollars are spent wisely, public services are delivered effectively, and political favoritism is permanently rooted out of federal operations.

Action Seven: The Government Accountability Act - 100% Truth & Transparency in Government

All government officials shall be legally required to provide full, truthful transparency in all public communications. Government employees who are caught lying, misleading the public, or manipulating information shall be immediately terminated and prosecuted. No more hiding behind "national security" to justify secrecy, only the Department of Defense shall have authority over classified information. Mandating full truth and transparency from government officials would end the culture of deception, cover-ups, and manipulation that erodes public trust. By enforcing immediate termination and prosecution for lying or misleading the public, and restricting classified information strictly to national defense matters, this reform would restore honesty, accountability, and rightful citizen oversight over their government. No more government lies. No more cover-ups. No more deception.

Action Eight: The Legislative Integrity Clause - End Corruption in Lawmaking

All bills must be limited to a single issue, no more massive bills stuffed with unrelated policies.

No bill shall exceed 100 pages, congress must fully read and debate every law they pass.

All bills must be authored by congress, not lobbyists, corporations, or special interest groups.

Congress shall be banned from trading stocks or financially benefiting from their position.

No more unreadable bills. No more backroom deals. No more corrupt legislation. Limiting legislation to a single issue, banning massive unread bills, and prohibiting lobbyist-written laws would restore integrity, clarity, and accountability to the lawmaking process. Requiring Congress to fully read and debate every bill and banning members from profiting off their office would end backroom deals, eliminate corrupt legislative practices, and ensure laws are written for the people, not for special interests.

Action Nine: The Election Integrity Clause - Secure America's Elections

All votes shall be cast in person, on Election Day, using paper ballots. Voter ID shall be required for all elections, no exceptions. Mail-in voting shall be strictly limited to deployed military personnel and legally disabled citizens. Election results shall be publicly counted and verified at every step. No more ballot harvesting. No more fraudulent mail-in votes. No more rigged elections. Securing elections through in-person voting, voter ID requirements, strict limitations on mail-in ballots, and public ballot verification would restore trust, transparency, and legitimacy to America's electoral system. By eliminating opportunities for fraud, ballot harvesting, and manipulation, this reform ensures that every legal vote is counted, every illegal vote is rejected, and the will of the people is protected without compromise.

Action Ten: The Legislative Powers Clause - Stop Executive & Bureaucratic Overreach

Only legislatures may pass laws, unelected bureaucrats and regulatory agencies shall be stripped of all lawmaking / regulating power. No governor, mayor, or local official shall have the power to impose mandates, restrictions, or policies outside legislative approval. Regulations must be passed through Congress or state legislatures, no more unelected officials dictating laws. Stripping unelected bureaucrats and executive officials of lawmaking power would end government by decree and restore constitutional lawmaking authority to elected legislatures. This reform ensures that no regulations, mandates, or restrictions can be imposed without direct approval from representatives accountable to the people, protecting individual rights and preventing executive and bureaucratic tyranny. The government will no longer rule by decree, only elected legislatures can make laws.

Action Eleven: The Right to Learn Clause - Reclaiming Education from Political Indoctrination

All public schools must teach U.S. history, civics, mathematics, science, and financial literacy.

Any school teaching anti-American or anti-constitutional ideologies shall be permanently shut down. Teachers found engaging in political indoctrination should be banned from the profession. Reclaiming education from political indoctrination would restore the core mission of public schools: Teaching objective history, civics, and essential skills. By banning anti-American propaganda and permanently removing teachers who engage in political indoctrination, this reform would protect students' right to a truthful, empowering education rooted in constitutional principles, ensuring future generations are equipped to preserve freedom and self-governance. No more rewriting history. No more Marxist indoctrination. No more anti-American propaganda.

Action Twelve: The Anti-Bureaucracy & Equal Education Clause - End Union Control Over Our Schools. Each state shall have one education department and one standardized curriculum, no more bureaucratic layers. School boards and teachers' unions shall be permanently abolished to prevent ideological corruption. Ending union control and collapsing bureaucratic layers in education would eliminate ideological corruption and political activism from the classroom. By establishing a single education department and standardized curriculum per state, this reform would ensure that schools return to their true purpose, teaching essential knowledge and skills, while protecting students from manipulation and restoring parental and state authority over education. The primary role of schools will be education, not political activism. Schools will teach, not indoctrinate.

Action Thirteen: The Anti-Grooming Act - Protecting Children from Sexual Exploitation

All forms of sexual education shall be banned in K-12 schools. Teaching gender ideology, transgenderism, or sexual orientation topics to minors shall be strictly prohibited. Banning sexual education, gender ideology, and transgender indoctrination in K-12 schools would protect the innocence of America's children and return the responsibility for sensitive topics to parents where it belongs. This reform draws a clear line against grooming, exploitation, and political manipulation of minors, ensuring that schools are places of learning, not arenas for sexual and ideological agendas. Any institution or individual that violates this sacred trust will face swift prosecution. Children will no longer be targets for political experimentation, they will be protected, respected, and allowed to grow free from adult-driven agendas.

The Bottom Line: This is The People's Revolution Over Government Tyranny

The era of career politicians, corporate-controlled elections, reckless spending, rigged voting, and bureaucratic tyranny ends here. This is not just a reform; it is a complete takedown of the corrupt system that has hijacked our Republic. Political parties will be stripped of their stranglehold. Government corruption will be exposed and dismantled. Congress will be forced back into the hands of the people it was created to serve. No more masters in Washington. No more elites ruling from the shadows. The Constitution will reign supreme, and the people will take back what is rightfully theirs. This is the beginning of the next American Revolution. And this time, we finish the job.

Act Four - Restoring Justice & Law Enforcement Integrity

For the United States to remain a free and just society, governed by the people and for the people, our judicial system must strictly adhere to the Constitution. Over the past century, the corrupt judiciary has been weaponized by political elites, especially the Democratic Party, to circumvent the legislative process and impose their radical agenda through judicial fiat. Judges no longer interpret the law, they create it. Prosecutors have abandoned impartial justice, and law enforcement has been politicized, manipulated, and restrained to serve corrupt politicians rather than protect the people. This act will restore integrity to our judicial system, ensure equal and fair justice for all, and restructure law enforcement to serve the Constitution rather than political interests.

Action One: The Presumption of Innocence Clause

Pre-conviction plea agreements shall be prohibited, no person shall be punished without a full trial. Guilty until proven innocent ends here, the burden of proof is on the government.

Prosecutors shall be prohibited from coercing plea deals with excessive sentencing threats.

Judges shall have no power to block the defense from presenting evidence. Restoring the true presumption of innocence and ending coercive plea deals would protect citizens from government intimidation, wrongful convictions, and abuse of prosecutorial power. By requiring full trials and guaranteeing the right to present evidence, this reform ensures that justice is based on truth and due process, not fear, manipulation, or threats from the state. The government will no longer be able to intimidate citizens into unjust convictions.

Action Two: The Accountability Clause

Any government official, including judges and prosecutors, who knowingly violate a citizen's constitutional rights shall be permanently disqualified from public service. Government officials shall not be protected by the Fifth Amendment in matters of misconduct. Holding judges, prosecutors, and all government officials personally accountable for violating constitutional rights would eliminate the culture of immunity and corruption within the justice system. By permanently disqualifying offenders and removing Fifth Amendment protections for misconduct, this reform ensures that those entrusted with power are never above the law and that the rights of the people are protected without exception. No more corrupt judges. No more rogue prosecutors. No more unaccountable government officials.

Action Three: The Anti-Immunity Clause

No government agency, public official, corporation, or private entity shall be immune from criminal or civil liability. All citizens shall have full due process rights to hold corrupt officials and corporations accountable. Abolishing immunity for government agencies, officials, and corporations would restore true equality under the law, ensuring that no entity public or private is above accountability. This reform empowers citizens to seek justice against corruption, negligence, and abuse, while ending legal protections that allow elites and powerful industries like Big Pharma to profit without consequence. Big Pharma shall no longer be shielded from liability for dangerous drugs and vaccines. No more legal loopholes for the elite. No more corporations profiting at the expense of human life.

Action Four: The People's Judiciary Clause

The judicial system shall be simplified, fully accessible, and free for all citizens to use without financial barriers. Equal legal representation shall be provided to all plaintiffs and defendants.

Private attorneys shall be prohibited from practicing in criminal, tort, and family law, ensuring all cases are handled fairly by court-appointed attorneys. Simplifying the judicial system and removing financial barriers would make true justice accessible to every citizen, not just the wealthy. By providing equal legal representation and prohibiting private attorneys from dominating critical areas like criminal, tort, and family law, this reform guarantees that outcomes are based on fairness and facts, not on who can afford the best lawyer. No more justice for the wealthy and injustice for the poor. No more rigged courts. No more legal manipulation.

The Judiciary's Systemic Failure: Criminal, Tort, and Family Law

The American judiciary has been corrupted beyond recognition, operating as an extension of elitist control rather than a defender of the people's rights. The wealthy and well-connected enjoy full protection under the law, while the average citizen faces an unjust system that exploits, abuses, and disenfranchises them.

Criminal Law: A System Rigged Against the Poor

The American criminal justice system is not broken, it is functioning exactly as it was corrupted to operate: Against the poor and powerless. Public defenders, buried under impossible caseloads, are reduced to plea brokers, not defenders of justice. Defendants without money are railroaded into pleading guilty, stripped of their right to a trial, and handed criminal records by a system that profits from their surrender. Meanwhile, the wealthy weaponize the system with high-priced lawyers who game the rules, manipulate judges, and buy favorable outcomes. Justice is not served in America; it is auctioned off to the highest bidder. Over 90% of federal convictions are secured through plea deals, not trials. Article III, Sec 2, Clause 3 states - The trial of all crimes, except in cases of impeachment shall be held by jury. This is not constitutional and it certainly is not due process; it is mass coercion under the guise of law. The United States does not lead the world in incarceration because it leads in crime. It leads because the courts, prosecutors, and lawmakers have built a machine designed to generate bodies for prisons and profits for the industries that feed on them. This is a war against the poor disguised as justice and poor minorities are the primary targets. Justice must no longer be a privilege of wealth or a punishment for poverty. It must be ripped from the hands of the corrupt and returned to the people it was sworn to protect. The days of blindfolding Lady Justice for the rich while turning her gaze on the poor must end, permanently.

Tort Law: Corporations Operate with Impunity

Today's tort system is a rigged battlefield where corporations use their vast financial resources to crush everyday citizens who dare to seek justice. Lawsuits filed against powerful companies are met with endless legal motions, delays, and escalating costs designed to bankrupt plaintiffs before a case even reaches a courtroom. Justice isn't determined by facts or fairness; it's determined by who can afford to fight the longest. The rich corporations win, not because they are right, but because they have the resources to outlast, outspend, and overpower the people seeking accountability. Under this reform, all tort cases will be handled through an equal-access, court-appointed system where wealth cannot be used as a weapon to obstruct justice. Every citizen will have a fair shot to bring a case, and corporations will be judged on the merits of the evidence, not on their ability to bury the opposition in legal fees. Big Business will no longer stand above the law. They will face the same courts, the same standards, and the same consequences as every American citizen they once sought to silence.

Family Law: Fathers' Rights Must Be Protected

For far too long, family courts have operated under a silent bias: presuming that fathers are less capable, less needed, and less important in the lives of their children. This systemic discrimination has torn families apart, driven countless fathers into financial ruin, and weakened the very foundation of our nation, "families". Family courts have been weaponized, turning custody battles into financial transactions where fathers are often treated as nothing more than a source of child support payments rather than vital parents. This ends now.

Under this reform, fathers shall have equal legal and physical custody of their children by default, ensuring that both parents are recognized as essential, not optional. Courts will be stripped of their ability to profit from broken families and will no longer assume that motherhood alone defines a child's best interest. Justice will be based on fairness, evidence, and the well-being of the child, not outdated stereotypes or financial incentives. Strong families create strong nations. The war on fatherhood ends here, and with it, the deliberate erosion of the American family.

Action Five: The Law Enforcement Reciprocity Clause

Law enforcement must exist to protect the rights of the people not to serve political agendas. Under this reform, the sheriff's, the only law enforcement officers directly elected by the people, will be restored as the highest legal authority within their jurisdictions. Sheriffs will operate independently, free from political interference by mayors, governors, or federal government. They will answer only to the Constitution and the citizens they are sworn to protect. Sheriffs and deputy officers across all agencies will be required to uphold the Constitution as their supreme duty, not the orders of corrupt politicians. Sheriffs will have full prosecutorial discretion over arrests within their jurisdictions, ensuring that local communities, not political operatives, determine what is just and lawful enforcement. Local, state, and federal law enforcement structures will be reformed and stripped of political manipulation. No longer will officers be forced to stand down while crime runs rampant to serve political optics. No longer will law enforcement be weaponized against political opponents while real criminals walk free. No longer will the trust between the people and those sworn to protect them be broken by backroom politics and corrupt agendas. True law and order will be restored. Law enforcement will once again serve the people, protect the

Constitution, and defend freedom without fear, without favor, and without political chains.

Reforming American Law Enforcement: Restoring Trust & Accountability

Policing in America has been hijacked by political agendas, corrupted by bureaucratic overreach, and turned into a tool of oppression rather than protection. Officers who once swore to uphold the Constitution have been caught between conflicting loyalties to the law and to the political powers that manipulate it for their own ends. The result is a devastating collapse of public trust, rising lawlessness, and a dangerous erosion of the very foundation of civil order.

The solution is clear and absolute: law enforcement must be removed from the grip of politicians and restored to its rightful role, serving and protecting the constitutional rights of the people. Officers must be held directly accountable for constitutional compliance, not political directives, ensuring that their loyalty remains to the law, not to corrupt officials seeking to exploit them.

Law Enforcement Must Protect Citizens, Not Political Interests

Under this reform, politicians shall be permanently prohibited from interfering with police operations. Never again will mayors, governors, or federal bureaucrats issue political stand-down orders that force officers to abandon citizens during riots, acts of violence, or mass shootings. Never again will law enforcement be handcuffed while innocent Americans are left defenseless. Sheriffs, as the highest constitutional law enforcement authority in each jurisdiction, will operate independently to enforce the law, maintain order, and protect life and property, free from political manipulation, coercion, or retribution. Law enforcement will once again serve the people, not the political elite. Officers will answer only to the law, to the Constitution, and to the citizens they swore to defend. The weaponization of police for political purposes ends here. The restoration of trust, accountability, and real justice begins now.

Ending Unconstitutional Policing Practices

The badge must never be a license for abuse. Yet across America, unconstitutional policing practices have become commonplace, officers fabricating probable cause, conducting unlawful searches, and prioritizing revenue generation over true public safety. Citizens are harassed over minor infractions while violent criminals walk free, eroding trust and undermining the very purpose of law enforcement. Under this reform, police shall be permanently prohibited from engaging in unlawful searches or manufacturing probable cause to justify arrests or citations. Any officer caught violating these principles shall face immediate removal and prosecution. Arrest quotas, ticket quotas, and any system that incentivizes harassment over protection shall be permanently banned.

Law enforcement's mission will be reset to its true purpose: prioritizing serious crimes that threaten life, liberty, and property, not shaking down the public over technicalities to feed bloated municipal budgets. No more police harassment over broken taillights while neighborhoods drown in drugs and violence. No more fines disguised as law enforcement while real criminals are ignored. The days of unconstitutional policing practices are over.

The people deserve protection, not persecution.

Strengthening Police Training & Standards

A badge and a gun demand the highest levels of discipline, skill, and judgment but today's standards for police training and recruitment fall dangerously short. To restore true professionalism to American law enforcement, we must raise the bar at every level.

Under this reform, all police officers will be required to complete elite-level tactical training focused not just on physical readiness, but on de-escalation, conflict resolution, and constitutional integrity. Physical fitness standards will be significantly raised, no more officers unfit for the demands of their duty. Intelligence and problem-solving abilities will become core requirements, ensuring that officers are prepared to think, adapt, and uphold their oaths under pressure. Every officer will also receive comprehensive training in constitutional law, civil rights, and due process making it clear that protecting the liberties of the people is not optional, but mandatory. Officers must know not just how to enforce the law, but why they enforce it, and whom they truly serve. Better training means better policing. Higher standards mean greater public trust. A professional police force, grounded in the Constitution and prepared to defend the people's rights, will be the new standard for American law enforcement.

Building Trust Between Law Enforcement & Black America

For over a century, Black America has suffered under a law enforcement system that too often served as a tool of oppression rather than a shield of protection. From the era of slave patrols to the abuses of Jim Crow, from targeted policing to systemic injustice, the wounds are deep and undeniable. The distrust between law enforcement and Black communities is not imagined, it is real, earned through decades of betrayal and abuse. True reform demands that we face this truth head-on. Empty slogans and political posturing will not heal the divide. The only way forward is through a total transformation of how law enforcement serves, protects, and engages with the communities it has too often alienated. The Constitution demands equal protection for all, and anything less is a betrayal of America's founding promises.

Restoring Urban Communities Through Law & Order

Our urban centers rich in culture, history, and potential have been devastated by unchecked crime, drug epidemics, and gang violence. These communities must be reclaimed, not through militarized policing or harassment, but through a restored partnership based on trust, respect, and constitutional policing. Sheriffs elected by the people and answerable to the people must take the lead. They must work directly with Black communities to rebuild trust at the ground level; walking the streets, knowing the residents, earning respect through action, not force. Law enforcement must be present not as an occupying army, but as partners in protecting families, children, and futures. Every citizen, regardless of race, deserves equal protection under the law.

Law enforcement must actively prove its loyalty to the Constitution by serving all Americans without bias, without discrimination, and without political agendas. Justice must be blind to color, but never blind to history. Only then can the cycle of mistrust be broken. Only then can strong communities and a stronger America rise in its place

Removing the Political Barriers to Real Change

For decades, the Democratic Party has deliberately divided America through racial and economic oppression. Black communities, in particular, have been targeted, kept in cycles of poverty, crime, and government dependency while being promised false hope and temporary relief in exchange for permanent political control. This betrayal is not accidental, it is systemic. It is the calculated result of policies designed to keep power centralized and the people divided.

That cycle ends here. Through real economic investment, authentic law enforcement reform, and direct community engagement, not bureaucratic lip service, Black America will finally achieve true liberation. True empowerment will not come from politicians handing out crumbs while consolidating power. It will come from rebuilding communities, restoring constitutional law, and returning dignity, opportunity, and safety to every American citizen. For America to thrive, all Americans must thrive. The chains of systemic oppression, whether economic, judicial, or political, must be broken completely and permanently. This act will dismantle the corrupt judicial system that has weaponized courts against the people.

It will restore law enforcement integrity by returning policing to the people it was meant to serve. It will ensure that every citizen, regardless of race, wealth, or political affiliation receives equal justice under the law. The rule of law must serve the people, not the powerful.

The Constitution must be upheld in every courtroom, every police department, and every government office without exception. Justice must once again be blind, fair, and unyielding to political influence. This is how America restores true law and order, not through slogans, not through empty reforms, but through structural, uncompromising change.

The Bottom Line: Justice Must Be Restored

No more corrupt judges. No more weaponized law enforcement. No more political interference in policing. No more oppression through unconstitutional courts. No more justice reserved for the powerful. The people demand and will have a system that defends liberty, not crushes it.

Act Five - Restoring State Sovereignty & Nullifying Federal Overreach

For the United States to truly function as a constitutional republic as it was designed the sovereignty of the states must be fully restored. The Founders understood that a centralized government, left unchecked, would inevitably grow into a monster of tyranny. That warning has come to pass. Today, the federal government has exploded beyond its constitutional limits, creating a bloated, unaccountable bureaucracy that infringes on states' rights, drains the national economy, and burdens every American taxpayer with trillions in reckless, wasteful spending.

The Tenth Amendment leaves no room for confusion:

"The powers not delegated to the United States by the Constitution, nor prohibited by it to the states, are reserved to the states respectively or to the people."

Yet Washington D.C. has steadily eroded that foundation, seizing authority over education, healthcare, agriculture, commerce, housing, and virtually every other sector of American life without any legitimate constitutional mandate. This act will draw a clear line. It will dismantle unconstitutional federal agencies that have no rightful place in the governance of a free people. It will return decision-making power to the states, where it belongs, closer to the people and responsive to their needs. It will slash trillions of dollars in federal spending, ending the debt-fueled bureaucratic empire that suffocates economic growth and individual liberty. The era of federal overreach ends here. The states will reclaim their rightful power. The people will reclaim their rightful sovereignty. And America will once again operate under the only system that can preserve liberty, a government limited, decentralized, and bound by the chains of the Constitution.

Action One: Terminate All Unconstitutional Federal Agencies

The federal government was created to be small, limited, and tightly bound by enumerated powers. Today, it has mutated into a sprawling, unconstitutional empire of bureaucracy, corruption, and waste. The Founders were clear: if the Constitution does not specifically grant a power to the federal government, that power belongs to the states or to the people. The Tenth Amendment reaffirms this principle without ambiguity. Yet Washington D.C. now illegally controls education, healthcare, agriculture, energy policy, environmental regulation, and even law enforcement domains that constitutionally belong to the states. This massive federal overreach has created a system of redundant agencies operating alongside state-level counterparts, wasting trillions of dollars, restricting freedom, and empowering unelected bureaucrats to impose their will on the American people without consent. The scale of the abuse is staggering: The federal workforce exceeds three million employees, costing taxpayers over $300 billion annually just in salary alone. Billions more are spent maintaining thousands of unnecessary federal buildings, fleets of millions of vehicles, bloated pension systems, and endless bureaucratic overheads. And for what? To create more red tape, more restrictions, and less liberty. Federal overreach isn't just unconstitutional, it is among the largest financial and political scams ever perpetrated on the American people. It siphons away the nation's wealth, suffocates innovation, tramples individual rights, and concentrates power into the hands of a few unaccountable elites in Washington. This reform will terminate all federal agencies operating outside constitutional authority. It will dismantle the layers of corruption that have buried the republic under bureaucracy. And it will return governance to the states and the people where it belongs. The chains that bind the federal government will be reforged.

And the American people will once again be free.

Action Two: Slash Federal Spending & End Trillions in Waste

The federal government is bleeding this nation dry. Today, Washington D.C. spends over $7 trillion annually, two trillion more than the combined budgets of all 50 states and every local government across the entire country. This astronomical figure doesn't reflect vital services or infrastructure improvements, it reflects bureaucratic bloat, political payoffs, endless waste, and corruption on a scale the Founders would have called treasonous. More than $3 trillion every year is squandered on bloated bureaucracies, unnecessary agencies, redundant programs, and outright fraud. This is not accidental; it is the natural consequence of a government that has outgrown its constitutional bounds and now exists primarily to sustain itself at the expense of the people. Meanwhile, America is suffocating under $36 trillion in national debt, a ticking time bomb that already costs taxpayers $1.2 trillion a year just in interest payments. That's over a trillion dollars annually thrown into a black hole that produces nothing, fixes nothing, and builds nothing for the future of this country. Washington D.C. has not just mismanaged our resources it has bankrupted our future. This is not incompetence, it is systemic corruption, and it has placed the American people, their children, and their grandchildren into debt slavery for generations to come. The only solution is total structural reform. We must slash federal spending back to constitutionally authorized limits. We must abolish the unconstitutional bureaucracy that feeds on taxpayer dollars and produces nothing but more control and more dependency. And we must restore fiscal responsibility by forcing Washington to live within its constitutional means just like every American family must live within theirs. The bleeding must end. The theft must end. The betrayal of the American taxpayer must end, permanently.

Action Three: End Federal Land Grabs & Restore State Control Over Land & Resources

One of the greatest, least discussed abuses of federal power is the massive, unconstitutional seizure of American land. Today, the federal government claims ownership of over 30% of all land in the United States, millions upon millions of acres wrongfully taken from the states and the people. These land grabs were never about protecting resources or ensuring public access. They were, and are, about control, control over agriculture, control over energy production, control over industry, and control over the very economic lifeblood of the states.

The Constitution could not be clearer.

Article IV, Section 3 strictly limits federal land ownership outside of the original territories. The federal government is permitted to own land only for military bases, post offices, and federal courts, nothing more. There is no constitutional authority for the federal government to seize vast stretches of land, restrict mineral rights, dictate environmental policies, or dominate state economies through regulatory strangulation. Through these illegal land seizures, Washington D.C. has weaponized land management to suppress energy independence, kill industries, destroy rural communities, and choke state economies into submission. It has used land control as a political weapon to enforce federal dominance over the states it was supposed to serve.

This reform will end the era of federal land theft. All lands wrongfully occupied or controlled by the federal government will be reclaimed by the states, placing authority back into the hands of the people who live on, work on, and depend on that land. States will once again control their own agriculture, energy, water, and mineral resources without interference from unelected bureaucrats in Washington. The government has no constitutional right to own the American West, to strangle state economies, or to dictate the future of local communities. The land belongs to the states. The resources belong to the people. And the federal government will be forced back inside the constitutional cage our

Founders built for it. The era of federal land theft ends here, and it ends for good.

Action Four: End Political Party Collusion That Weakens States' Rights

The two-party system has consolidated power, forcing state governments to bow to federal control rather than defend their sovereignty. State leaders prioritize political party loyalty over their duty to their own constituents. States must assert their independence, rejecting federal interference and restoring constitutional governance. Governors and state legislatures must be loyal to their constituents, not political party agendas dictated by Washington insiders.

Action Five: Restore the Founders' Vision of a Limited Federal Government

The Founding Fathers did not create a federal government to rule over the daily lives of Americans, they created a framework to protect liberty and preserve the sovereignty of the states. In the true American republic, the states govern themselves independently, each reflecting the will, culture, and needs of their own people, while the federal government was designed to perform only a narrow set of clearly defined functions. The Constitution enumerates only a few legitimate federal responsibilities:

- Providing for the common defense
- Conducting foreign affairs
- Regulating interstate commerce
- Maintaining postal services
- Establishing a federal court system

That's it. Everything else was intentionally left to the states or to the people. Yet today, the federal government has exploded into every corner of American life, controlling education, healthcare, agriculture, business regulation, environmental policy, energy production, and even local policing. This massive overreach is not just wrong, it is blatantly unconstitutional. Every state already possesses its own police forces, fire departments, schools, hospitals, roads, and energy infrastructure. There is no constitutional justification for the existence of bloated federal bureaucracies operating parallel to, and often overriding, state authority. There is no need for federal agencies to dictate how states educate their children, manage their hospitals, produce their energy, or protect their communities. The federal government was never meant to dominate American life. It was never meant to legislate culture, micromanage economies, or replace state and local governance with top-down control. It exists for one purpose only: To defend the nation, to protect liberty, and to provide a simple framework for the states to cooperate as a union of free peoples, not as subjects of a central empire.

This reform will restore that original vision of our Founders. It will strip away the unconstitutional powers seized by Washington D.C. It will return the sovereignty of the states and the freedom of the people. And it will remind the federal government of the truth the Founders built into the Constitution itself: It is the servant of the states and the people, not their master.

Action Six: The Single Layer of Government Clause

Government in America was never meant to be a maze of overlapping bureaucracies, conflicting authorities, and endless layers of red tape. The Founders envisioned a republic where power was limited, divided, and kept close to the people, not layered so deeply that accountability would disappear. Yet today, government exists in bloated layers, federal, state, county, city, regional agencies, all fighting for power, duplicating efforts, wasting resources, and confusing the very people they claim to serve. This must end. Under this reform, government shall exist at only one level in any capacity where governance is needed. No more dual bureaucracies competing for authority over the same functions. State governments shall have exclusive authority over all domestic policies, education, healthcare, law enforcement, agriculture, infrastructure, energy, and social services within their own borders.

The federal government shall be limited strictly to its constitutional roles: defending the nation, managing foreign affairs, regulating interstate commerce, operating a postal service, and maintaining a court system. Nothing more. This will eliminate the overlapping, redundant bureaucracies that waste trillions of taxpayer dollars, generate conflicting regulations, and fuel constant power struggles between federal and state governments. It will force clarity, accountability, and efficiency back into the structure of American governance. One layer of government per function. No more bureaucratic pileups. No more endless finger-pointing and evasion of responsibility. No more hiding behind layers of government to dodge accountability. The government closest to the people, the states will govern daily life, while the federal government will be chained back to its rightful, limited purpose. This is how we restore order, sanity, and liberty to the American system of governance. And it is how we end the era of bureaucratic tyranny once and for all.

The Financial & Economic Benefits of Ending Federal Overreach

Eliminating unconstitutional agencies will save taxpayers trillions of dollars annually.

Reduced government spending amounts to lower inflation, reduced national debt, and stronger economic growth. States will be free to enact policies that best serve their people without federal interference. Private sector job creation will skyrocket as businesses are freed from burdensome federal regulations. Washington's stranglehold on our economy has crippled America, this plan will unleash its full potential. The Bottom Line: Restoring State Sovereignty Is the Only Way to Save the Republic. No more unconstitutional federal agencies. No more multi-layered bureaucracies wasting trillions. No more federal land grabs and economic interference.

No more power-hungry politicians dictating policies to the states. The states were meant to govern themselves; it's time to return power to the people where it belongs. The Constitution is clear. The federal government has stolen power for far too long. It's time to take it back. This is how America restores true liberty and self-governance.

Act Six - Media & Big Tech Reform

Malcolm X once warned, "The media is the most powerful entity on earth. They have the power to make the innocent guilty and to make the guilty innocent." His words ring truer today than ever before. In modern America, the corporate media and Big Tech giants have become the most dangerous instruments of propaganda, misinformation, and societal control. No longer independent, no longer objective, they now operate as full partners with the Washington bureaucracy, manipulating public perception, covering up government corruption, silencing dissent, and shaping reality itself to serve their globalist masters. The corporate media has abandoned any pretense of journalism. It does not report the truth, it manufactures narratives designed to protect the political elite, preserve the deep state's power, and push anti-American, globalist policies onto an unsuspecting public.

This same corrupt media apparatus selectively inflames racial tensions by exploiting isolated police encounters in Black communities, fueling riots, destruction, and deeper national division, while ignoring daily violence that claims far more lives. It censored the truth about COVID-19.

It suppressed overwhelming evidence of election fraud. It waged a relentless, coordinated disinformation campaign against President Donald J. Trump, culminating in the Russia collusion hoax, a deliberate lie that wasted millions in taxpayer dollars and paralyzed the duly elected government of the United States. Big Tech is equally guilty, the media spreads the lies, and Big Tech ensures that truth is erased. They control the flow of information, rig search results, silence dissenting voices, shadow-ban citizens, and deplatform anyone who challenges their narratives. Together, the media and Big Tech have rigged elections, deepened political and racial divisions, and actively worked to undermine the constitutional foundation of the American Republic. This is not merely a political disagreement, it is a coordinated assault on the very concept of free speech, free thought, and representative government. The only path forward is bold and uncompromising. The media and Big Tech must be stripped of their power to deceive, censor, and manipulate. New laws must be enacted to permanently dismantle their monopoly over information. Strict penalties must be imposed for censorship, collusion with government agencies, election interference, and disinformation campaigns targeting the American people. Without real accountability, the First Amendment is dead. Without real reform, the Republic itself cannot survive. The time has come to end the era of propaganda and censorship, forever. The American people will reclaim the truth. And with it, they will reclaim their country.

Action One: Pass the Truth in Media Act

The First Amendment protects free speech, but it does not protect fraud, defamation, or organized deception. For too long, corporate media entities and so-called journalists have hidden behind free speech protections while knowingly spreading lies, destroying reputations, and manipulating the American public with politically engineered narratives. This has not been journalism, it has been propaganda, weaponized against the people. Under the Truth in Media Act, journalism will once again be held to a legal standard of truth and integrity. Any media organization, journalist, anchor, or corporate executive found knowingly spreading false information or colluding with political figures, government agencies, or foreign entities to manipulate public perception, shall face criminal prosecution. There will be no more legal immunity for organized lies. Mandatory prison sentences will be imposed for each count of convicted misinformation, ensuring real consequences for those who betray the public trust.

Every false story deliberately planted, every reputational hit job launched, every political conspiracy waged through the media will now carry the weight of criminal liability.

The corporate media has abused its position of influence for decades, lying with impunity, slandering private citizens and public figures alike, fueling division, protecting corrupt power structures, and sabotaging honest democratic discourse. Those days will be over.

The threat of prison, not just lawsuits, not just public backlash, but prison will force a return to honest journalism, where facts are verified, sources are real, and the American people receive the truth they deserve, not the propaganda someone paid for. No more corporate mouthpieces. No more media monopolies of deception. Truth will be restored, and with it, trust.

Action Two: Pass the Communications Integrity Act

The First Amendment was not written to protect speech the government agrees with, it was written to protect speech the government, the elites, and the powerful would rather silence.

In today's America, Big Tech corporations have illegally assumed the role of speech police deleting posts, banning users, manipulating algorithms, and silencing dissent, not just on their own, but often in direct collusion with government agencies. This is nothing less than an assault on the constitutional rights of the American people. Under the Communications Integrity Act, Big Tech platforms will be permanently prohibited from censoring content in any form.

Every post, article, video, image, and communication shared online will be fully protected under the First Amendment, just as if it were spoken from a town square. No private corporation, regardless of its size, wealth, or political allegiance, will have the power to silence, restrict, deplatform, shadow ban, or interfere with political discourse or the free flow of information.

If any company engages in censorship, manipulates political narratives, or colludes with any government official or agency to suppress information: Their FCC and FTC licenses will be immediately and permanently revoked. Their corporate protections will be stripped away.

Their executives and responsible officers will face criminal prosecution, with zero tolerance for infractions. The First Amendment does not end where Silicon Valley begins. The Constitution does not grant corporations the authority to erase speech. It does not empower tech oligarchs to control elections, shape political debates, or silence the citizens they claim to serve.

Censorship is tyranny. And tyranny must be destroyed. The era of corporate thought control is over. The people will reclaim their voice, and with it, they will reclaim their Republic.

Action Three: Investigate & Dismantle Corrupt Media & Tech Giants

The media and Big Tech corporations are not just biased, they are active participants in the corruption and destruction of the American Republic. They have colluded with government officials to suppress the truth, spread coordinated propaganda, interfere in democratic elections, and silence citizens who dared to speak against the establishment narrative. This is not journalism. This is not business. This is treason against the people they were meant to inform and serve. Under this reform, any media or technology corporation found guilty of colluding with political officials to manipulate public perception or suppress vital information shall be forcibly disbanded. Their FCC and FTC licenses will be permanently revoked.

Their executives and employees involved in election interference, COVID disinformation campaigns, and mass censorship operations will be criminally charged and banned for life from working in journalism, media, or communications industries. All assets, all properties, and all revenue generated by these corrupt corporations will be seized and redistributed to the victims of censorship, election interference, and reputational destruction. Those who sought to control the nation by controlling information will be held personally and financially accountable.

The media and Big Tech have caused irreparable harm to the fabric of this Republic.

Their influence must be eradicated with the same ruthless determination they used to spread lies, sow division, and manipulate the future of our nation.

The Bottom Line: The era of media lies & big tech censorship ends. No more corporate propaganda. No more government-controlled narratives. No more election interference. No more unconstitutional censorship. No more media deception designed to divide and weaken America. The media and Big Tech declared war on the truth, on free speech, and on the American people, and this is the way we fight back. This act will permanently dismantle the media's power to manipulate. It will restore truth, defend free speech, and protect future generations from ever being subjected to tyranny by lies, deception, and censorship again.

Good does not prevail by waiting politely. Good prevails when it fights back with the same or greater force that evil uses against us. The battle for truth, free speech, and journalistic integrity begins now. And this time, the people will win.

Act Seven - Establishing the National Association of Sheriffs (NAS) as a Permanent Government Policing Authority.

The first and most sacred duty of any government is to protect its citizens and to ensure that justice is applied equally, impartially, and without political bias. Thomas Jefferson, one of the principal architects of American liberty, captured this truth perfectly when he wrote: "The most sacred of the duties of government [is] to do equal and impartial justice to all its citizens." Yet today, the institutions tasked with fulfilling that sacred duty, specifically, the Department of Justice (DOJ) and the Federal Bureau of Investigation (FBI), have betrayed their mission. They no longer serve justice. They no longer serve the Constitution. They serve only themselves and the corrupt political establishment they were supposed to keep in check. The DOJ has been entirely politicized, operating not as a neutral defender of the law, but as a weaponized enforcer for the Democratic Party and the entrenched Washington elite. They shield their own while crushing their political enemies.

They protected Hillary Clinton, allowing her team to destroy subpoenaed evidence devices, smashed with hammers, emails erased without facing a single meaningful consequence.

They buried overwhelming evidence of Biden family corruption, Hunter Biden's criminal activities in Ukraine and China, and Joe Biden's direct involvement choosing cover-ups over accountability. They actively participated in treasonous acts, orchestrating Spy-Gate and the Russia collusion hoax in an attempt to overthrow a duly elected President, Donald J. Trump.

They have repeatedly trampled the Constitution violating due process, attacking free speech, persecuting political dissidents, and treating America First patriots as enemies of the state.

The DOJ and FBI are no longer neutral arbiters of justice, they have become instruments of tyranny, using unchecked power to protect the political elite and crush law-abiding American citizens who dare to oppose them. This must end. It will end.

To restore true justice and constitutional law enforcement, the National Association of Sheriffs (NAS) will be commissioned as the permanent government policing authority answerable not to political parties or bureaucrats, but to the Constitution and the people. The NAS, composed of sheriffs elected directly by the people, will assume the role the DOJ and FBI have long since forfeited: Protecting individual rights. Investigating government corruption. Enforcing the law impartially, regardless of political status, wealth, or influence. Under the NAS, no elite criminal will be shielded. No innocent citizens will be persecuted. No law will be selectively enforced based on political allegiance. The era of weaponized federal law enforcement is over.

The Constitution will reign again. Justice will once more be equal, impartial, and unyielding as it was always meant to be.

Action One: The Republic Defense Clause

To preserve liberty, justice, and the integrity of the Republic, the United States must establish a permanent, constitutionally grounded law enforcement authority that answers to the people, not politicians. Under this reform, the National Association of Sheriffs (NAS) will be formally commissioned as the permanent government policing authority tasked with protecting the Republic from internal corruption and lawlessness at every level of government.

The NAS will be federally funded as a top national security priority, recognizing that the greatest threat to the Republic is not foreign enemies, it is the rot of corruption within our own institutions. Through a democratic process, all sheriffs throughout the United States shall vote to form the National Association of Sheriffs High Council, which shall be entrusted with the authority to appoint and expel leadership responsible for investigations of public officials.

The NAS will consist of One-Million sheriffs and deputy members, distributed strategically across all 50 states to ensure maximum coverage, accountability, and immediate operational readiness. No act of government corruption will go unpunished. Every violation of the Constitution will be investigated. Every abuse of power will be exposed. Every betrayal of public trust will be prosecuted to the fullest extent of the law.

This reform will set a permanent, unbreakable precedent: There will be ZERO TOLERANCE for crime in government, regardless of rank, wealth, political affiliation, or status.

No longer will elites operate under a separate system of justice. No longer will the American people be subjected to a system that shields the powerful and punishes the innocent.

The message will be clear: If you seek to serve in government, you must serve under the law, not above it. The era of unaccountable political corruption ends with the rise of a people's law enforcement authority dedicated to the Republic, the Constitution, and the people themselves.

The National Association of Sheriffs (NAS) will be the shield of the Republic.

And corruption will be crushed under its watch.

Action Two: The Tyranny Defense Clause

To defend liberty and restore true constitutional governance, the National Association of Sheriffs (NAS) will be granted full oversight and operational authority over the Federal Bureau of Investigation (FBI). An immediate and sweeping purge of all corrupt, compromised, and non-compliant FBI personnel will take place. Every agent, analyst, and employee will be subject to rigorous vetting. All remaining personnel will be retrained under strict constitutional standards.

The mission of federal law enforcement will be completely redefined: investigating and prosecuting government corruption, not persecuting political dissidents. The NAS will assume control of all FBI buildings, resources, equipment, and operational assets. No corrupt infrastructure will be left standing. No political machinery will be left intact. The NAS will wield full investigative and arresting powers over all elected officials, appointed bureaucrats, and government employees at every level, federal, state, and local. No one will be immune.

No office will be untouchable.

The NAS High Council, through a democratic majority vote, will have the constitutional authority to expel any government official found guilty of violating their sworn oath to support and defend the Constitution. This will apply to all public servants without exception: politicians, bureaucrats, judges, agency heads, no one will be shielded by title or power. In addition, the Department of Justice (DOJ) will be radically restructured, its bloated size slashed, and its authority strictly confined to its original constitutional purpose: administering justice for the people, not wielding justice against the people. No more political prosecutions. No more selective enforcement based on ideology. Never again will the DOJ or FBI be weaponized against American citizens. The era of unchecked government corruption, bureaucratic tyranny, and deep state treachery is over.

The Bottom Line: Restoring Justice & Ending Government Tyranny

No more politically motivated prosecutions. No more election interference by corrupt law enforcement agencies. No more government officials operating above the law.

No more deep state weaponization of justice. The DOJ and FBI have betrayed the Republic, colluding with corrupt politicians, abusing their power, and waging an open war against the Constitution and the American people. Their treachery must be met with swift, unrelenting, and decisive force. The National Association of Sheriffs (NAS) will become the enforcers of TRUE JUSTICE. They will ensure that every government official, from the highest levels of Washington to the lowest offices of local government, is held fully accountable to the law, without exception, without bias, and without political interference.

Government must once again fear the people, not the other way around.

With the establishment of the National Association of Sheriffs as America's constitutional policing authority, the power is returned to its rightful owners: We the People.

The days of bureaucratic tyranny are over.

The days of constitutional justice have begun.

REVOLUTION BLUEPRINT

5

VETERAN, PATRIOT AND BIKER COALITION

T he Cause: A tyrannical government has overstepped its constitutional limits, violating state sovereignty and infringing upon the unalienable rights of the people. By exceeding its enumerated powers, it has trampled the Constitution, ignored the Tenth Amendment, and betrayed the trust of the American people.

The Resolve: Veterans and citizen patriots are called to form a powerful coalition, one million men strong, committed to defending liberty, restoring constitutional governance, and holding those in power accountable. In the spirit of 1776, the Sons of Liberty must rise again, just as our Founding Fathers once did, to fulfill our sacred civic duty. We, the people, must hold our public officials accountable, compelling them to honor their sworn oaths to uphold and defend the Constitution.

Article VI, Section III of the U.S. Constitution states:

"The Senators and Representatives before mentioned, and the members of the several state legislatures, and all executive and judicial officers, both of the United States and of the several states, shall be bound by oath or affirmation, to support this Constitution."

This Oaths Clause is the foundation of the people's authority to reclaim our republic. Any government official who has violated their sworn duty to protect and uphold the Constitution has, by their own unconstitutional actions, disqualified themselves from their office. They can be, and they should be removed from public service. It is time to restore the republic and ensure that those entrusted with power remain true to the principles upon which this nation was founded. The people are the masters of all government. Our power does not come from bureaucrats, it comes from our Creator, as boldly declared in the Declaration of Independence:

"We hold these truths to be self-evident, that all men are created equal, that they are endowed by their Creator with certain unalienable rights, that among these are life, liberty, and the pursuit of happiness. That to secure these rights, governments are instituted among men, deriving their just powers from the consent of the governed. That whenever any form of government becomes destructive of these ends, it is the right of the people to alter or abolish it and to institute new government."

The Founding Fathers not only established the people's supreme authority over government but also ensured our ability to defend it. The Second Amendment explicitly affirms: "A well-regulated militia, {**being necessary**} to the security of a free state, the right of the people to keep and bear arms shall not be infringed."

The Declaration of Independence and the Second Amendment together form the foundation of our mission. They are the lifeblood of our duty to stand as a constitutional, well-regulated militia, a patriot coalition empowered to resist tyranny and preserve the security of our republic. True liberty endures only when patriots stand ready to defend it. The time has come to shake the tree of liberty and answer the call to action. Veterans, patriots, and bikers, united together under the one banner, "the Sons of Liberty" one million men strong. Together, we shall stand committed to restoring constitutional order and ensuring that tyranny never again takes root in our land. The time to act is now, any man that may consider serving in the patriot coalition or to take part in its mission, let him first reflect on the extraordinary failure of our Republic. We are witnessing a government that has betrayed its people, facilitating an invasion at our borders, spending billions of taxpayer dollars through NGOs to aid and abet the mass influx of fighting-age males from across the globe into the interior of the United States. At the same time, our elected officials send billions more to foreign nations, not for the benefit of the American people, but to secure the borders of other countries while leaving our own borders defenseless. These are acts of treason, and as patriots, we must recognize the gravity of this betrayal. But the corruption does not stop at the border. The same cabal of traitors has seized control of our elections, ensuring that the will of the people is overridden to serve their own interests. Given this unmistakable reality, no patriot can conclude anything other than the United States government is fully compromised, no longer representing the best interests of its citizens, but serving the ambitions of an entrenched ruling class, the permanent bureaucracy they created. Let each man read for himself the Declaration of Independence and fully embrace the remedy prescribed by the Founding Fathers for ridding our government of tyranny and treason. It is not an act of rebellion; it is the lawful and constitutional restoration of power to the people.

To be clear: We are not overthrowing the government, nor are we engaging in insurrection. The American people are the rightful masters of all government, we cannot overthrow what is already ours. No man can overthrow his own house. What we are doing is reclaiming control, through demanding the resignations and terminations of those who have violated their sworn oath to support and defend the Constitution. Reclaiming the Republic is a call to action. We cannot allow corrupt politicians and their propaganda driven media to control the narrative of our mission. We must be bold. We must be unwavering. We must speak the truth. Our Founding Fathers made it clear: when a government engages in a long train of abuses, trampling the Constitution and endangering the future of the Republic, it is not only the right but the duty of the people to remove it. Our mission is rooted in the Constitution, guided by the same 1776 blueprint that secured our independence from tyranny. The steps we take to restore constitutional governance and expel those who have betrayed their oath mirror the unwavering resolve of our forefathers. This is the Spirit of 1776, reignites, 250 years later. The brave are called once more. You are the brave patriots of today, this is your calling. The time to unite is now. The Fate of Our Nation Hangs in the Balance. We can no longer prioritize civility over survival, not when the very foundation of our Republic is at stake. There is no civility in communism, just as there will be none in globalism. The enemies of freedom do not play by the rules of honor, nor will they willingly surrender the power they have seized. We are not voting our way out of this; no politician is coming to save us. The only path forward is the unification of veterans, bikers, and patriots into an unstoppable force, "the Sons of Liberty" Patriot Coalition. This is our last and only hope to preserve liberty and restore constitutional order. The mere presence of a million plus patriots standing united under one banner is enough to strike fear into the hearts of tyrants. This is in fact their greatest fear, a force greater than any they could marshal against us, a force that will not bow to their corruption or intimidation. Their resignations will be their surrender. Their removal and arrest will be the alternative. The people yield the ultimate power over government. In our unity, our power is undefeatable.

Our mission is clear: bring together all patriot platforms and groups into a single, unstoppable front. By forming a powerful coalition, we unify countless organizations under the shared cause of restoring our constitutional republic. Each group retains its unique purpose, but together, we become exponentially stronger. As millions stand united, every initiative gains momentum, every effort is reinforced, and every voice grows louder. Our strength lies in our numbers. Our ability to mobilize, rally, and demonstrate our unstoppable force is critical. It is this collective power that will strike fear in the bureaucrats who have abused their public offices. United, we cannot be ignored. Together, we will restore the Republic. The Unstoppable Force is America's Patriot Bikers No force on God's earth rallies in greater numbers for patriotic causes than American bikers. Our unwavering commitment to freedom, strength in our numbers, and fearless resolve make bikers the driving force in the fight to reclaim our Republic.

To succeed, we must mobilize tens of thousands of biker patriots across the states, creating a powerful, coordinated presence that cannot be ignored. Imagine one million patriot bikers, united under one banner, with a single chain of command, a force of liberation, an unbreakable front against tyranny. This is the movement that will shake the foundations of those who have seized power. This is the unstoppable army of freedom, "The Sons of Liberty"

The Sons of Liberty: The Vanguard of the United States Militia will serve to: Remove oath-breakers from all government and hold them accountable, Support and promote an Article V Convention of States to restore constitutional governance and establish a just government that serves the people, Protect and defend our elections from corruption and ensure the integrity of the democratic process. The Sons of Liberty will stand as the defenders of the Republic, committed to upholding the Constitution and securing the future of our nation.

Mobilizing America's patriot bikers - The Methodology

To build a force of this scale rapidly and ensure immediate mission readiness, we must first establish a well-regulated structure with a clear and respected chain of command. Every member must recognize and uphold this hierarchy with absolute respect and unwavering loyalty. The Sons of Liberty Biker Coalition (SLBC) must extend across the entire continental United States, capable of mobilizing tens of thousands of patriots in short order to demonstrate strength whenever and wherever necessary. This requires a robust network of chapters with a stringent vetting process, ensuring every member is trustworthy, committed, and battle-ready.

Building the Well-Regulated Component:

This begins with uniting patriot bikers and military veterans nation-wide under one banner, a coalition of hardened, disciplined, and fearless Americans who stand ready to defend the Republic. The key to mobilizing this force lies in a fundamental truth: Bikers are America's patriots. We love God, Family, and Country, the very foundation of American patriotism. And today, all three are under attack. The American Bikers will rally for their country and forge the largest biker coalition in the world. A disciplined, organized force with a command structure rivaling our nation's military. Strength is in numbers, and building a force over a million bikers strong demonstrates the people's power to end tyranny. The Sons of Liberty Biker Coalition must be built on this foundation. Corrupt government officials act without fear of the people, but that will soon change. Imagine hundreds of thousands of armed, disciplined biker patriots, united under a single chain of command, demonstrating our strength in overwhelming numbers. This is the force they will fear. There is no faster, more effective way to deploy tens of thousands of men to a single location in short order than on motorcycles, the mechanical horse of our time. History has already proven the power of this strategy. The Rolling Thunder Freedom Ride has brought hundreds of thousands of patriot bikers through the streets of D.C. every year, standing as a powerful testament to who we are and what we stand for. Another Historic Display of Biker Patriotism occurred with the Two Million Bikers to D.C. rally that proved just how powerful a united force of patriots could be. Hundreds of thousands of bikers mobilized in record time, assembling in the nation's capital to defend American honor. The rally was born out of outrage and defiance. On the anniversary of the attack on 9/11, an Islamist group planned to march on D.C. to celebrate what they saw as a victory, the destruction of the Twin Towers and the loss of 3,000 American lives. But patriot bikers weren't about to let that happen. In a stunning display of raw patriotism, bikers from across the country rode in mass formations, shutting down highways, flooding D.C., and completely overshadowing the enemy's plans. We made it clear: America's warriors would not stand idly by while radicals insulted our nation and its fallen. Baltimore native, Top-Fuel Bill, was the visionary behind Two Million Bikers to D.C. His leadership and determination brought together a million bikers in the greatest act of biker patriotism in history. The Two Million Bikers to D.C. rally was a powerful demonstration of what patriot bikers can accomplish. It proved that America's bikers are the backbone of any large-scale mobilization effort. This is why they are vital to our cause today. Now, we call upon the same proud warriors who rode in Two Million Bikers to DC, those who once stood in defense of our nation's honor. This time, we ride not just for pride, but for the very survival of our Republic. The battle-cry will echo once more, rallying hundreds of thousands of veterans and patriots to stand united in this historic fight.

Biker = Brotherhood, The Force, The Militia

The Sons of Liberty Biker Coalition will operate like any well-regulated MC, with a single, disciplined chain of command and an unbreakable brotherhood binding its members together. Millions of patriot bikers and veterans across this country are fed up. Politicians and bureaucrats are actively destroying our Republic from within, trampling the Constitution and betraying the people they swore to serve. But we honor our Founding Fathers' instructions on dispelling tyranny, and we accept our civic duty to act. Wherever you go, the Sons of Liberty will be there. This nationwide presence is the final piece in the strategy of uniting bikers across the country to form the largest biker coalition in the world, serving as the well-regulated militia, empowered by the very Constitution our forefathers fought to establish. An Unrivaled Force with a Strategic Advantage

The biker coalition is built on three fundamental pillars: Brotherhood, a bond that cannot be broken. Uncompromising loyalty - absolute commitment to one another and the mission.

Respect for the chain of command - a disciplined, structured force that spans all 50 states, giving us an instant geographical advantage unmatched by any other movement.

Once this coalition is fully formed, we will be a force to be reckoned with. And above all, brotherhood means loyalty, All for One, and One for All. Uniting patriot bikers and veterans under a single command, with one mission, to enforce the terms of the Constitution, is the only hope to truly save our country. The time to be brave is now.

S.O.L Biker Coalition Structure: A Disciplined Force for Constitutional Enforcement

Command & Leadership: Twelve Presidents will lead the twelve regional chapters of the coalition, each overseeing operations across multiple states. A National President/Commander will serve as the thirteenth leader, unifying the entire movement under a single chain of command. Each chapter will appoint a Vice President and a Sergeant-at-Arms, ensuring continuity and stability in leadership. Building the Infrastructure for a Well-Regulated Militia. Uniting America's patriot bikers and veterans immediately establishes a structured command system with built-in loyalty, discipline, and operational efficiency. Chapters will be responsible for vetting and managing the influx of veterans and patriots joining the movement, ensuring that only the most committed and honorable individuals take the oath. The twelve regional chapters will work together to develop national infrastructure, ensuring the coalition achieves mission-ready status as quickly as possible. Their primary task will be to organize, train, and mobilize forces while maintaining the logistical framework needed to operate at a national level.

Mission Readiness & The Oath to Defend the Republic: The national objective is to achieve full force readiness to execute its primary mission: removing oath-breakers and traitors from government. The coalition will be composed exclusively of military veterans and patriots, all of whom will take a sworn oath to defend the Constitution and the Republic against all enemies, foreign and domestic. However, most importantly, all members will swear an oath to each other: "All-for-One, and One-for-All" (AFO/OFA). This unbreakable bond means that an attack on one member is an attack on us all. If any Sons of Liberty member is unjustly detained by the government, the entire organization will mobilize to secure their release, at all costs. AFO/OFA

The Mission: Constitutional & Peaceful, But Resolute

Our mission is clear: to peacefully and constitutionally remove those who have betrayed their oaths and committed treason against our Republic. However, if the government chooses to strike first, weaponizing its agencies against the coalition or its members, those responsible will be immediately removed from public service for violating their oaths.

We are fully aware that permanent Washington controls political offices and government agencies across all fifty states. The potential for government retaliation is real, and it could come from federal, state, or local authorities. This is why the twelve MC chapters will establish a dominating presence in every state of the Union, ensuring that we can respond swiftly and decisively should the government attempt to suppress our movement. While our goal is to avoid conflict, any interference in our constitutional mission will not be tolerated. Law enforcement and the military must recognize the constitutional power of the people and remain neutral until the mission is complete and constitutional order is restored. Respect for Law & Military Institutions: We respect the institution of law and the U.S. military. The very reason for our existence is the government's failure to uphold that same respect. Our overwhelming strength in numbers will force local agencies to acknowledge, respect, and ultimately support our cause.

Tactical Operations & Special Forces Units

The twelve MC chapters will be composed of military veterans and patriot citizens, with each chapter covering approximately four states. Each chapter will form an elite tactical special forces unit, composed of the most highly trained veterans and patriots with extensive military and tactical experience. These specialized teams will be tasked with potential high-priority tactical missions, while the broader force will stand ready to provide overwhelming support when needed.

Our goal is to build the largest citizen force in history, committed to restoring constitutional order and ensuring that the Republic remains in the hands of the people. Our greatest barrier is complacency. There is no shortage of patriot bikers brave enough and passionate enough to engage. The complacency lies in the false hope the politicians will end their corruption. Tyranny never ends itself. We must break this illusion and confront our reality. A major barrier to our mission is the deeply ingrained belief that electing "good Republicans" can save the country. This is a fatal misconception, and we will confront it head-on. The best way to dismantle this flawed theory is through open dialogue on every available platform. When presented with logic and historical truths, patriots will realize that the Republican Party is just as much the enemy of the people as the Democratic Party. The Republican and Democratic Parties are not even public institutions, they are privately owned entities controlled by the central banking cartel, big business, and foreign adversaries, not the American people. Many Americans already recognize this, but millions remain trapped in the two-party illusion, believing it is the natural way our government was designed to function. This is false. The two-party system is the antithesis of a representative republic and is a tool of control, not governance. Political alliances foster corruption, elected officials take an oath to the Constitution, but they also pledge allegiance to their party. The parties dictate policy, and elected officials vote accordingly, not based on what serves their constituents. The two political parties are mere fronts for the global financial elite, big banks, corporations, and foreign interests. Campaign financing, SuperPACs, and lobbying have transformed Congress into a marketplace where policy is bought and sold to the highest bidder. Elected officials don't even read the bills they vote on anymore; they simply follow orders from their party leadership.

Why "Electing Good Republicans" Is a Dead-End Strategy:

The establishment will always protect itself, no matter how many "outsiders" get elected, the system will neutralize them. Fair elections are a myth, rigged primaries, election fraud, and media manipulation ensure outsiders never gain real power. The national debt will never be reduced, spending will never be cut, and taxation theft will never be eliminated, because the system was designed to serve its masters, not the people. President Trump and D.O.G.E. will face as much opposition from the Republican Party as they will the Democrats. Except the Republicans will pretend like they are in support of Trump all while working to obstruct him. The enemy is the two-party system owned by the central bank globalist elites. They control both parties, and through them, they control every political office, judicial bench, and government agency across the country. These are the true puppet masters, the weaponized force behind the curtain. They do not respect our Constitution; they are actively dismantling it. And the Republican and Democratic Parties are the facilitators of this destruction. The permanent bureaucracy will never surrender power peacefully the deep state has entrenched itself in every level of government and will never allow "fair elections" to decide their fate. For 50+ years and over 30 election cycles, Americans have believed they could vote their way out of tyranny. Yet, the country has only suffered greater harm. The path to saving the Republic does not lie in electing "good people" into a corrupted system. The system itself must be dismantled. The only way forward is through: Nullification of all unconstitutional acts of overreach, Eliminating political alliances from government entirely, and re-establishing a Constitutional Republic that enforces its own limits on power. To achieve this, every Sons of Liberty member and supporter must be fully committed to the mission. There is no middle ground. America has been asleep for too long. The belief that "we just need to elect better people" has been a four decade-long failure. The two-party system is a trap, the government is captured, and the globalist elite are in full control. The coalition of veterans and patriot bikers will be the force that breaks this system apart. Our mission is clear. Our purpose is justified. Our time is now.

"Fortune always favors the brave."

God bless the USA, the Constitutional Militia, and our mission to restore the Republic!

6

Rise of the Christian Patriot - A Call to the Brave

Dear Christian Patriots,

A fundamental flaw exists in the way we think about defending our faith in America. The church in this nation has been infiltrated by weak-minded, left-leaning pastoral leadership. For decades, left-wing progressives have indoctrinated young adults through higher education, and our pastors are no exception. They, too, have spent years absorbing progressive propaganda, and as a result, their worldview has been shaped by the same forces that have sought to erode the foundation of our Christian values. The consequences of this indoctrination are evident: left-wing progressivism produces passive, timid men who lack the strength to stand against adversity. Sadly, many of our pastors fit this mold, leading the church in weakness and teaching Christian men to be docile in the face of mounting hostility.

The Battle Against Secularism

America is home to people of many faiths: Christians, Jews, Buddhists, Muslims, agnostics, and atheists. Among them, a vocal and aggressive segment of atheists works tirelessly to erase God from public life. These godless activists have succeeded in removing prayer and Christian teachings from our schools and government institutions. Yet, despite recognizing that the absence of God has led to moral decline, Christians have done little to stop it. The reason? A church led by spineless leaders, unwilling to fight for their faith. Where was the church when schools stopped praying? Where was the resistance when God was removed from government spaces? Rather than rise in defiance, too many Christian leaders chose silence, allowing secular forces to dictate the terms of public discourse. This failure to act is a betrayal of our faith and an abdication of our duty as believers. When state and local governments shuttered churches under the guise of COVID-19 emergency policies, most pastors complied without resistance. They embraced draconian mandates, closing their doors and forcing congregations to wear ineffective masks. These shutdowns had no constitutional authority, the First Amendment guarantees the free exercise of religion. Yet, the church cowered, submitting to unconstitutional edicts without question. While most churches bowed to tyranny, a few brave pastors resisted. In places like Baltimore, Florida, New Jersey, and Tennessee, these leaders refused to close their doors. They stood firm, recognizing that the fight was not just against government overreach but against the very forces of evil seeking to suppress Christianity. These men embodied the spirit of David against Goliath, proving that courage and faith could overcome even the most formidable opponents. The battle we are facing is not just about church closures or public prayer, it is part of a greater war waged against Christianity and liberty itself. The same globalist forces responsible for orchestrating the September 11 attacks and enacting the overreaching Patriot Act are the ones who weaponized the COVID-19 pandemic to further expand government control. Their goal is clear: to dismantle national sovereignty, establish a one-world government, and obliterate religious freedom. Both the Democratic and Republican parties have been infiltrated by these globalists, working behind the scenes to erode

American values. Their corruption knows no bounds, and their ultimate aim is the destruction of our Republic. If they succeed, religious freedom will cease to exist in America. Persecution will follow, and the Christian faith will be driven underground. The time to act is now, before it is too late. The battle of good versus evil is not some distant, future event, it is happening now. The forces aligned against us seek to destroy everything we hold sacred. But we are not powerless. We were made in God's image, with strength and courage instilled in our very being. The time has come to reclaim our role as warriors for Christ. Throughout scripture, God raised armies to fight against evil. The Bible is clear: we are not called to be passive. We are called to stand, to fight, and to defend our faith. Those who have led you to believe that Christianity requires surrender to the world's corrupt forces have deceived you. God calls us to surrender to Him alone, and in doing so, we are empowered to resist evil with unwavering faith.

My Testimony: God's Purpose Revealed My own life is a testament to the power and purpose of God. I have faced near-death experiences, including an aortic aneurysm and a terminal diagnosis of congestive heart failure. But through divine intervention, my life was spared, not just once, but multiple times. My doctors were astounded, calling my recovery a miracle. I know without a doubt that God has a purpose for me, just as he has a purpose for you. If you are reading this, then you too, feel the calling. You are not here by accident. God is awakening the warrior within you. It is time to shake off the pacified version of Christianity that weak leadership has instilled. The real battle is before us, and we must be prepared to face it. This war is not just physical,. it is spiritual. And the most powerful weapon we have is prayer.

God has given us a promise in 2 Chronicles 7:14:

"If my people, which are called by my name, shall humble themselves, and pray, and seek my face, and turn from their wicked ways; then will I hear from heaven, and will forgive their sin, and will heal their land."

This is our moment to come together in prayer, to seek God's face, and to ask for His divine intervention. I call upon all Christian Americans to unite in prayer every single day at 3:16. Wherever you are, set your alarms and pray at precisely 3:16 in your time zone. Pray alone or when possible, pray in groups. "For where two or three gather in my name, there I am with them." (Matthew 18:20) Millions of voices raised in prayer will be a force that no evil can withstand. We are at a crossroads. Will we continue to cower in fear, or will we rise as the mighty warriors God created us to be? The time for complacency has passed. The forces of darkness are moving swiftly, but with God on our side, we will not be defeated. "If God is for us, who can be against us?" (Romans 8:31)

Christian Patriots, it is time to rise. It is time to stand united. With faith as our shield and prayer as our weapon, we will reclaim our nation for God.

The Future Belongs to the Brave

God bless you all. Stand strong, stand faithful, and RISE UP!

THE HEALTHCARE RESOLUTION

This chapter serves as a testament to the American people that there is absolutely a better way to approach healthcare, one that does not necessitate government intervention. Healthcare remains one of the most pressing concerns that must be addressed in the New Republic. Currently, the federal government has assumed near-total control over our nation's healthcare system. The extent of this interference became painfully evident during the COVID-19 pandemic, as federal mandates dictated hospital policies, further cementing government overreach. In the New Republic, the federal government will function strictly within its enumerated powers, and healthcare management is not among them. That authority rightfully belongs to the states. The Healthcare Resolution presents a pragmatic and sustainable solution, one that ensures healthcare access for all while dramatically reducing the exorbitant costs associated with Medicaid, Medicare, and federal healthcare subsidies.

Healthcare in America has been seized by the federal government and manipulated for political purposes. Once regarded as the gold standard worldwide, albeit with areas for improvement, America's healthcare system was significantly disrupted by the passage of the Patient Protection and Affordable Care Act (Obamacare). This legislation inserted the federal government into every facet of healthcare, effectively placing bureaucrats between doctors and their patients. In addition to imposing a sweeping array of regulatory burdens, Obamacare mandated that all citizens obtain health insurance through government-controlled exchanges, expanded Medicaid to an unsustainable level, and prohibited insurance companies from denying coverage. It also required all plans to offer a broad spectrum of universal benefits, regardless of individual needs or circumstances. The cumulative effect of these mandates has been catastrophic: hospitals and providers are now more regulated and controlled than ever before.

The destructive consequences of this federal overreach were fully exposed during the COVID-19 pandemic, as hospitals and providers were coerced into enforcing irrational and anti-scientific policies dictated by federal agencies. With the federal government shouldering the lion's share of medical expenditures, spending over $1.5 trillion annually on Medicare, Medicaid, and other subsidized healthcare programs, hospitals have become financially dependent on compliance with government mandates. As a result, these institutions are no longer driven by the principle of patient-centered care but instead by adherence to bureaucratic dictates. This has led to a sharp decline in care quality while costs continue to escalate. The Congressional Budget Office (CBO) projects that total healthcare expenditures in 2026 will reach a staggering $4.3 trillion, an increase of $2 trillion from 2015. Moreover, government healthcare subsidies alone have doubled, surging to $1.8 trillion and accounting for 45% of the CBO's total projected healthcare expenditures.

Several key factors are driving this unsustainable inflation in healthcare costs. Chief among them are the excessive regulations imposed by Obamacare, which have burdened hospitals and providers with crushing administrative and compliance requirements. These obligations have significantly inflated operational costs, forcing healthcare facilities to devote more resources to bureaucracy than to patient care. Hospitals and medical providers now grapple with overwhelming administrative workloads, from navigating complex insurance billing processes to managing cumbersome federal compliance regulations.

Insurance providers, too, wield disproportionate power over the healthcare system. Positioned between patients and healthcare providers, they receive a steady influx of premium payments from policyholders, allowing them to function with minimal financial risk. Like any other corporation, insurance providers operate with profit margins in mind, setting their rates based on expected costs while seeking to maximize revenue. However, the unpredictability of medical needs creates a fundamental challenge: insurers cannot foresee when, how, or why individuals will require treatment. Likewise, they cannot accurately predict the level of care a physician will deem necessary for a given patient. This uncertainty incentivizes insurance providers to introduce cost-cutting measures that often compromise patient care while padding their bottom lines.

The current healthcare system is unsustainable and deeply flawed, having been transformed into a bureaucratic nightmare by federal overreach and corporate interests. The New Republic must reclaim the foundational principle that healthcare should be driven by patient needs and physician expertise, not by government dictates and insurance company profit motives. The Healthcare Resolution lays the foundation for a system that is efficient, cost-effective, and centered on the well-being of the American people.

Insurance companies exert significant influence over healthcare costs and delivery in the United States. Their practices, aimed at controlling expenses, often have unintended consequences that affect both providers and patients. Insurance companies employ various strategies to manage costs, such as setting reimbursement rates, requiring prior authorizations, and conducting utilization reviews. While these measures aim to prevent unnecessary spending, they can also lead to increased administrative burdens for healthcare providers and potential delays in patient care. Notably, the U.S. healthcare system is unique among industrialized nations in allowing private insurance companies to profit from managing citizens' medical care. This profit-driven model contributes to higher administrative costs and overall healthcare expenditures. Delays in insurance reimbursements are also a significant concern. Data indicates that 31% of inpatient claims submitted to commercial insurers were not paid for over three months, compared to just 12% for those submitted to traditional Medicare. Such delays strain healthcare providers' finances and can impact their ability to deliver timely care. Additionally, the requirement for prior authorizations can hinder patient access to necessary treatments. This process often leads to postponed or denied care, potentially compromising patient outcomes.

The administrative complexity introduced by insurance companies is but another contributing factor to higher healthcare costs. Private insurers in the U.S. have administrative costs that consume about 14% of premiums, significantly higher than the administrative costs associated with government-run programs like Medicare. Furthermore, the profit margins of health insurance companies have seen substantial growth. Since the passage of the Affordable Care Act, the top five U.S. health insurers have accumulated over $371 billion in profits, with UnitedHealth Group alone accounting for a significant portion of this increase. The current dynamics between insurance companies, healthcare providers, and patients have led to a system where financial considerations often overshadow patient care. This environment has sparked discussions about the need for systemic reforms, including proposals for universal healthcare models that prioritize patient outcomes over profits. While insurance companies play a role in managing healthcare costs, their practices inadvertently contribute to higher expenses and barriers to care. Addressing these challenges requires a comprehensive approach that balances cost control with the imperative to provide accessible, high-quality healthcare for all.

The other side of the equation is the stranglehold of the health insurance monopoly. Health insurance companies, like any other for-profit corporation, are designed to generate revenue, except their profits come at the direct expense of affordable, quality healthcare for Americans. Healthcare is a multi-trillion-dollar industry, and the insatiable greed of the insurance sector has made it one of the primary drivers of skyrocketing medical costs. Their never-ending pursuit of profit serves no purpose other than to inject unnecessary costs into our healthcare system. The only parties that should be profiting from healthcare are those who actually provide it, hospitals, physicians, and medical professionals, not bureaucratic middlemen leeching off both patients and providers. Insurance companies exist solely to extract profit, further complicating the direct relationship between doctor and patient. Their interference bloats costs, drags out payment processes, and restricts patient care. This convoluted system is entirely unnecessary, so much so that every other industrialized nation has outright rejected it. There is no logical reason to pay an insurance company thousands of dollars annually just for the privilege of having them dictate what treatments you can and cannot receive. Yet, Americans have been conditioned to believe that this system is indispensable because it has been ingrained into our society for over half a century. But everything that has a beginning can also have its end, and it is time for this disastrous system to be dismantled. The real question isn't whether the insurance model should end, The question before us is what do we replace it with.

A New Era in American Healthcare: The Revolution Blueprint isn't just a roadmap for restoring our Republic, it's a battle plan to reclaim our healthcare system from decades of corruption, inefficiency, and fraud. Just as we aim to dismantle the political machine that's hijacked our government, we must do the same with healthcare, a system rigged against both patients and providers. Let's be clear: one of the first casualties in this overhaul is Obamacare. The so-called Patient Protection and Affordable Care Act was never about protecting patients or making care affordable. It was a calculated, unconstitutional power grab, a gateway to government-controlled healthcare disguised as reform. At the same time, it handed massive profits to insurance corporations, turning health coverage into a racket while millions still struggle to access care. Obamacare will be abolished completely and unapologetically. The Revolution Blueprint will expose the truth behind this legislation and restore the constitutional boundaries that were trampled in its passage. But this isn't just about repealing a law. It's about ripping the healthcare system out of the hands of corporate monopolies and government bureaucrats and returning it to the people. In the new model, doctors and patients reclaim control, medical decisions made at the bedside, not in boardrooms or bureaucratic offices. No more predatory billing practices. No more insurance gatekeeping. No more government-mandated care under the illusion of protection. The time for band-aid solutions is over. The Revolution in healthcare starts now. And it starts by building a system from the ground up, transparent, accountable, and rooted in liberty.

Before we move forward, we must confront a simple truth: Americans purchase health insurance primarily to protect themselves from catastrophic medical emergencies. It was never meant to cover every check-up, cold, or prescription, it was designed as a safeguard against financial ruin in the event of a serious illness or accident. This is no different than how we treat car insurance. We're required to carry it not for oil changes or tire rotations, but for collisions and unexpected damage. With over 150 million vehicles on U.S. roads and only a small percentage involved in accidents each year, we all still pay premiums based on the risk of the rare, but costly, event. The same logic applies to our health: out of 330 million Americans, only a fraction suffer catastrophic health events in any given year. Now imagine if car insurance were forced to cover oil changes, new brakes, engine tune-ups, and every maintenance task in between. The cost of coverage would explode. That's exactly what has happened to health insurance. We've expanded it to cover predictable, routine services, doctor visits, screenings, flu shots, even minor prescriptions, and now wonder why premiums, deductibles, and out-of-pocket costs have skyrocketed. At its core, insurance is about the transfer of risk protecting against unpredictable, high-cost events in exchange for a manageable premium. When insurers are forced to absorb the cost of every basic, foreseeable medical expense, they raise premiums accordingly, not to serve the people, but to maintain profit margins. If health insurance were limited to what it was originally designed for, catastrophic emergencies, most Americans would see dramatically lower costs. But instead, we're forced to pay thousands per year for coverage that doesn't even kick in until after inflated deductibles are met, and all while the quality of care continues to decline.

So why does this irrational system persist? Because it was built to serve the insurance industry, not the American people. With the full backing of the federal government, health insurance has been manipulated into a bloated, monopolized system that maximizes profit for insurers while trapping both patients and doctors in an endless web of bureaucratic red tape. We've been sold a lie: that this system is the only way to ensure access to healthcare. In reality, it's one of the largest financial scams in American history. As of 2023, U.S. healthcare spending reached $4.9 trillion, nearly 18% of the GDP, far more than any other industrialized nation, yet outcomes and access continue to lag behind. Health insurance was never meant to be a payment plan for everyday care. It was meant to protect against devastating loss. Over time, it has been weaponized against us. The Revolution Blueprint doesn't just expose this truth, it offers a path forward. One where patients reclaim control, doctors practice medicine without corporate interference, and the cost of care is determined by free market principles, not profit-driven collusion. It's time to sever the chains of this insurance-driven stranglehold. The revolution in healthcare is coming. And with it, a new model, one that finally puts the American people first.

The Cost of Obamacare: How the American People Were Betrayed

Under the crushing weight of Obamacare, millions of Americans face an impossible choice, pay outrageously high premiums or gamble with their health and go uninsured. Increasingly, hard-working families are choosing the latter, not because they don't care about their health, but because health insurance, even with government subsidies, has become financially unsustainable. Let's talk facts. Since the Affordable Care Act was signed into law in 2010, the average annual premium for an individual plan on the federal exchange increased from $2,784 in 2013 to over $5,700 by 2017 and now exceeds $7000 in 2024. While subsidies cushion the blow for some, millions make just enough to disqualify them from meaningful assistance, trapped in the middle, paying full freight for insurance that often delivers minimal value until a high deductible is met. It's not just individuals. Small businesses, which provide nearly half of all private-sector jobs in America, are dropping employee coverage at alarming rates. According to the Kaiser Family Foundation, fewer than 31% of small firms now offer health benefits, down from over 40% just two decades ago. Why? Because they can't afford it. Premiums for employer-sponsored plans have risen 47% in the past decade alone, strangling the very backbone of the American economy. And here's the hidden truth: the entire insurance industry is propped up by employer-based coverage. If businesses stopped offering health insurance, the entire system would collapse. Most Americans never see the full cost of their plans, it's automatically deducted, subsidized, and baked into their compensation packages. But if they had to physically write the check each month, the overwhelming majority would walk away. Even now, over 27 million Americans remain uninsured, not all because they're poor. Many are making a deliberate choice. They see through the scam. They understand that health insurance today is little more than a bloated, overpriced middleman offering poor value outside of major emergencies. These Americans are not being reckless, they're being rational. They pay out-of-pocket for routine care, skip the monthly extortion, and take their chances on a system that's failed them. The myth that insurance is necessary for routine medical care is just that, a myth. It was manufactured to keep the public locked into an inflated system designed for profit, not care. The truth is simple: insurance was meant to cover catastrophic events, not every minor sniffle or check-up. And yet, Obamacare expanded the scope of insurance to include everything, creating a system where insurers rake in billions while patients get crushed under co-pays, deductibles, and surprise bills. We were told Obamacare would fix the system. Instead, it weaponized it. This was never about affordable care; it was about control. And now, as the system buckles under its own weight, the American people are waking up.

The Revolution Blueprint calls for nothing less than a total reset. It's not just about ending Obamacare. It's about ending the lie.

The Two-Tiered System: What Insurance Companies Don't Want You to Know   At the core of our healthcare crisis lies a deliberately concealed truth; there are only two levels of care that matter, primary care (routine, minor medical needs) and major care (hospitalization and emergencies). And the uncomfortable truth is this; we only need insurance for one of them. Before Obamacare restructured the market and handed power to mega-insurers, many Americans, especially self-payers and indepen-dent brokers, understood the value of a two-part coverage model.

Policy A: Covered routine doctor visits, screenings, prescriptions, and minor illnesses, everything you can predict and typically budget for.

Policy B: Covered catastrophic events, surgery, intensive care, cancer treatment, and other life-threatening emergencies.

Here's where it gets damning; Policy B was cheap. Catastrophic-only insurance used to cost just a few hundred dollars a year. Why? Because the probability of a major claim was extremely low. The overwhelming majority of Americans will go their entire lives without ever being hospitalized for a life-threatening condition. Insurance companies know this. That's why the "major medical only" model was a low-cost, high-efficiency product, too effective, in fact, for the corporate parasites who saw more profit in mandatory, comprehensive coverage. By forcing everyone into bloated plans that cover every minor interaction with the medical system, flu shots, physicals, blood tests, sinus infections, insurance companies guaranteed themselves a windfall. Because when you cover everything, you can charge for everything. And here's the real kicker, insurance is supposed to be a risk-transfer mechanism, not a prepayment system. Everyone pays in, and only a small fraction should ever need a payout. That's how insurance stays affordable. But when you start covering predictable, routine, low-cost care, it's no longer insurance, it's legalized extortion wrapped in red tape. When insurers began absorbing everyday expenses, they began hemorrhaging money. But did they reform? Cut costs? Reduce overhead? Of course not. They passed the bill to us, jacking up premiums across the board, inflating deductibles, and locking Americans into contracts that deliver less and cost more every year. And all of this, under the guise of "affordable care."

Why do they get away with it? Because the health insurance industry isn't just powerful, it's politically untouchable. A trillion-dollar empire with a grip on Washington. These corporations have bought and paid for the very lawmakers charged with regulating them. The same politicians who pretend to serve the people are the ones writing laws that serve the insurers. They've created a government-backed monopoly, where insurance companies set the prices, dictate the payment rules, and weaponize the billing system against both patients and providers. This is not a free market. It is a rigged system, by design. And the people profiting off that design are the same ones telling you it's the best we can do. The Revolution Blueprint rejects that lie.

The American people have suffered long enough under a system that was never built to serve them. The Revolution Blueprint delivers a bold and uncompromising plan to overhaul our nation's healthcare model, not reform it, replace it. This is not about tweaking the edges of a corrupt machine. It's about tearing it down and building something fundamentally better in its place. We will abolish the exploitative insurance model that profits from pain and thrives on confusion. We will eliminate the bureaucratic interference that inserts government and corporate middlemen between doctors and patients. And we will restore what always should have been sacred: a direct, private, and accountable relationship between provider and patient. Under this new system, the cost of primary care will drop dramatically. Why? Because we are cutting out the parasitic middleman, the insurance corporations that inflate costs and add no value. Routine healthcare will finally be affordable, transparent, and accessible to every American. No more pre-authorizations. No more denied claims. No more medical decisions made by paper-pushers in insurance offices. That era is over. Insurance companies, their lobbyists, and their bought and paid for politicians no longer get a seat at the table. Their stranglehold on our healthcare system is finished. The future of American healthcare belongs to the people, not to profiteering conglomerates, and certainly not to the bureaucratic overlords in Washington who have hijacked the system for political gain.

The next chapter in healthcare isn't government-run and it isn't insurer-owned, it's membership-based. The Revolution Blueprint proposes a shift to Healthcare Membership Networks (HCMs) a streamlined, insurance-free model where Americans pay directly into a network of trusted providers in exchange for full access to care. No third parties. No billing games. No surprise statements. This model would unite physicians across specialties into a single, coordinated system, offering every member comprehensive care, from annual checkups to specialty services, for one affordable monthly fee. The groundwork for this healthcare system is already in place. Across the country, large physician groups and medical institutions like Johns

Hopkins and Mercy Physician Centers have established community-based models where patients receive a wide range of services; diagnostics, cardiology, lab work, podiatry, optometry, wellness programs, all under one roof. This is the future, and it's already functioning.

Even outside of these major hubs, thousands of doctors operate within referral-based networks, sharing patient care and medical records while maintaining independence. The infrastructure exists. The transition to membership-based care would be seamless, because the only thing missing is the freedom to cut out the insurers. Insurance companies serve a single function in the healthcare system, billing. That's it. They don't provide care, they don't heal patients, they process payments and take their cut. So, if we're serious about removing them from the equation, we must replace the billing model that keeps them in power. The truth is, solving America's healthcare crisis doesn't just require better coverage, it requires a complete redefinition of how we pay for care. The financial model must be rebuilt from the ground up.

Redefining the Financial Model: Healthcare as a Service, Not a Gamble While the structure of medical care would remain intact, the billing model would be radically transformed.

Part A: The network of physicians, specialists, and community care centers already in place.

Part B: A membership-based payment system, modeled after health clubs, where Americans pay a predictable monthly fee for unlimited access to medical services. Just like a gym membership gives you access to the full range of equipment, classes, and amenities, a healthcare membership would give you access to diagnostics, general practice, chronic condition management, and preventive care, all without the delays, denials, or deductibles. The model works. It ensures consistent revenue for providers, keeps costs transparent, and guarantees members can get the care they need when they need it. This isn't a dream. This is a revolution grounded in reality. And it's already within reach.

Let's Break Down the Financials; To understand the power of the membership model, just look at a mid-sized gym. With 10,000 members paying $50 per month, it generates $500,000 in monthly revenue, or a staggering $6 million per year. That kind of consistent cash flow provides stability, profitability, and scalability, all without relying on government grants or billing insurance companies. Now apply that exact same concept to healthcare, a physician network operating under a membership-based model would enjoy the same predictable, recurring revenue, but without the administrative chaos that comes with insurance billing, claim denials, pre-authorizations, and delayed reimbursements. Patients would pay a flat monthly fee for unlimited access to primary and preventive care, no surprise bills, no bloated premiums, no middlemen skimming profits from both sides of the transaction.

The result? A massive increase in operational efficiency and a system that actually works, for both patients and providers. Just like a health club doesn't collapse under the weight of every member showing up at once, healthcare networks function on the same principle of staggered demand. Not everyone visits at the same time. Not everyone needs care every week. The usage is naturally distributed, daily, weekly, monthly, allowing these networks to serve large populations without being overwhelmed. Physicians already see a fixed number of patients per day. Larger centers, like those modeled after Johns Hopkins or Mercy Physician Centers, operate as multi-practice hubs, with physicians referring patients internally for diagnostics, labs, imaging, and specialty care, all within one facility. The system already exists. It works. It's efficient. The only thing broken is the billing system, because of the insurance middlemen. Remove them, and what you're left with is a lean, direct, and patient-centered care model. No bloated bureaucracy. No predatory price gouging. Just care, delivered when and where it's needed, backed by sustainable, community-driven financial support. And here's the best part, everything required to implement this system already exists. The infrastructure is in place. The physicians are ready. The referral networks function. The only thing missing is the will to cut out the insurance cartels and put power back in the hands of the people and the doctors who serve them.

What Changes Under the Membership Model? Just One Thing: Who Gets Paid Under this membership-based healthcare model, the entire structure of care remains intact, doctors still diagnose, treat, refer, and heal. Hospitals still operate. Clinics still serve their communities. The only thing that changes is how they get paid. Gone are the mountains of insurance paperwork. Gone are the endless claim denials and the maddening calls for pre-authorization. Gone are the inflated billing codes, hidden fees, and surprise invoices. The bureaucratic nightmare vanishes, and with it, the insurance companies' power to stand between you and your doctor. For decades, we've been told that healthcare cannot function without insurance companies, that they're essential to making the system work. That is a lie. A manufactured myth, pushed by an industry that profits off suffering and has no interest in wellness, only in wealth. Here's the truth, we do not need insurance companies to manage our care. We never did. The real infrastructure, the providers, the networks, the technology, already exists to support a direct-pay, membership-based system. The only thing standing in the way is the insurance cartel that has bought off our politicians and rigged the law to protect its monopoly. Eliminate them, and what's left is a system that works; Doctors are paid directly and fairly Patients know exactly what they're paying for. Care is restored to a relationship, not a transaction. Administrative overhead, currently consuming up to 25–30% of every healthcare dollar, gets slashed. Costs drop. Access improves. And control returns to where it belongs, the patient and their doctor. This revolutionized healthcare model doesn't just challenge the status quo, it destroys it. It dismantles the corrupt, government-backed insurance racket that has been bleeding our healthcare system dry for decades. The days of bureaucrats and insurance executives controlling your care are over.

The people are taking it back. The future of American healthcare is transparent, efficient, affordable, and finally accountable to the public it serves.

The Future of Healthcare: A Membership-Based Model That Puts Patients First

The Healthcare Membership Model (HCM) isn't just a new idea, it's the inevitable next step in delivering affordable, efficient, and high-quality care to every American. This system is built on a simple but powerful foundation, patients choose their physician network, and providers compete to earn and keep their membership. That means better service, lower costs, and continuous innovation driven by real competition, not mandates or monopolies. Imagine a flat monthly membership fee of $150 per person for primary care access. Multiply that by the U.S. population of 350 million (citizens and non-citizens alike), and the total national expenditure would be: 350 million × $150/month × 12 months = $630 billion per year

Now compare that to what we're spending today, in 2024, the average monthly premium for employer-sponsored single coverage is $746, with family plans averaging over $2,100 per month. That's $8,951 per year for an individual, and $25,572 per year for a family, and those figures don't include deductibles, co-pays, or out-of-pocket costs. Overall, the U.S. spends more than $4.9 trillion annually on healthcare. $1.7 trillion of that comes directly from the federal government for Medicare, Medicaid, and CHIP programs that fail to provide timely, affordable care for millions. By comparison, a $150 flat monthly fee, just 20% of today's average premium—would deliver core care to every American and immediately cut costs across the board. This model doesn't just save money, it obliterates waste.

And the savings don't stop there. In 2023, America spent over $978 billion on primary care and clinical services. But it's estimated that 25–35% of that total was consumed by insurance-related administrative overhead: billing departments, coding systems, paperwork, claim denials, appeals, audits, and pre-authorization schemes. That's more than $300 billion in bureaucratic waste, gone the moment you remove the middlemen.

This is how we break the system:

- No premiums.
- No deductibles.
- No claim denials.
- No insurance gatekeepers deciding what care you can receive.

Instead, patients pay a predictable monthly membership fee. Doctors are compensated fairly and directly. States can subsidize care for low-income residents, cutting federal healthcare spending by over $700 billion annually and returning power to the states, where it constitutionally belongs. This is not some radical theory. It's modeled after real-world systems like Direct Primary Care (DPC) practices already operating across the country, proven, effective, and scalable.

$150/month isn't just possible, it's logical. In fact, it's a fraction of what we pay today to be denied care tomorrow.

How the Membership Model Works: The Healthcare Membership Model (HCM) operates on a simple, proven principle, just like a gym membership. Patients pay a flat monthly fee in exchange for unlimited access to core healthcare services. It's predictable. It's transparent. And it eliminates the confusion, complexity, and exploitation of the current insurance-based system. For just $150 per month per member, the HCM model covers:

- Unlimited primary care
- Routine checkups
- Preventive care
- Basic treatments and chronic care management
- Diagnostics, lab work, and basic imaging (e.g., X-rays, blood tests)

No deductibles. No co-pays. No claim forms. No surprise bills. Just care, direct, simple, and accessible. Each patient chooses their own healthcare network or physician group, just as they would a gym or wellness club. Once enrolled, they receive full, unlimited access to that network's services. No more waiting for insurance approval. No more fighting billing departments. The doctor-patient relationship is restored, uninterrupted by corporate gatekeepers.

Now flip the perspective, what does this model mean for physicians and healthcare facilities? Let's use a mid-sized physician center as an example:

100,000 patients enrolled at $150/month per patient = $15 million in monthly revenue, and $180 million in annual revenue. That's guaranteed, recurring, and predictable income, the kind that insurance-based models can't deliver. No delays. No denials. No reimbursement games. The impact is profound, more financial stability allows providers to invest in cutting-edge medical technology, staff expansion, and better facilities. Less administrative waste means doctors and nurses spend time on patients, not paperwork. Healthy competition between networks ensures higher standards of care, better patient experiences, and lower costs over time. In short, everyone wins except the insurance companies. This model doesn't just improve healthcare economics, it liberates the system. It frees doctors to practice medicine the way they were trained, and it gives patients control, clarity, and confidence in how their care is delivered.

Separating Primary Care from Major Medical: Restoring Sanity to the System

The brilliance of the Healthcare Membership Model (HCM) is in its simplicity, it finally separates primary care from major medical coverage, restoring the original intent of what insurance is supposed to be. Insurance was never designed to cover predictable, routine expenses. You don't use car insurance to pay for oil changes, tire rotations, or brake replacements. You use it when something goes seriously wrong, a collision, a breakdown, or a major mechanical failure. Health insurance should work the same way. Under the HCM system, your monthly membership covers all primary care services, checkups, diagnostics, preventative care, chronic care, and wellness visits. Major medical coverage becomes a separate, low-cost rider, reserved for rare but serious events: hospitalizations, surgeries, emergency room visits, and long-term illness management. Because major claims are statistically uncommon, these policies would be far more affordable than today's bloated insurance premiums.

How Employers Would Adapt

For the nearly 160 million Americans currently receiving employer-sponsored coverage, the transition is seamless. Employers would simply pay the employee's membership fee, just as they currently pay premiums. But the difference is revolutionary. Employees wouldn't lose their doctors when they change jobs. They wouldn't have to navigate a new insurance provider, reapply for coverage, or worry about pre-existing condition exclusions. Their membership stays with them, not their employer. The middleman is eliminated, and control returns to the patient. And for employers, this shift removes a massive administrative and legal burden, while offering a more affordable and predictable alternative to traditional plans. Everyone wins, except the insurance companies.

Government Assistance: State-Based, Not Federally Controlled For low-income Americans, the HCM model replaces federal programs like Medicaid with state-funded healthcare vouchers. Every eligible citizen simply enrolls in the network of their choice, and the state covers their membership cost. This eliminates federal bureaucracy, shrinks the size and scope of Washington, and brings healthcare governance back to the states, where it constitutionally belongs. Veterans would still access specialized care through the VA system, but basic primary care and local services could be delivered through community networks, reducing travel burdens and increasing access.

This is not a policy tweak. It's a total revolt against the insurance-driven racket that has corrupted American healthcare. Primary care and insurance should never coexist. Insurance should only cover unpredictable, catastrophic events. Government has no constitutional authority to control healthcare, it must return to the states.

By transitioning to this membership-based model, we can:

- Cut federal healthcare spending by 66%
- Slash national healthcare costs from $4 trillion to $1 trillion
- Eliminate insurance company interference
- Ensure universal access to affordable, high-quality care

This isn't theory. This is necessity. The insurance-industrial complex has drained the nation's wealth, dictated our care, and corrupted the relationship between doctor and patient. It's time for a revolution in healthcare, and The Revolution Blueprint provides the roadmap. The HCM model delivers more than reform, it delivers restoration. It provides universal access to primary care, slashes costs, and eliminates wasteful government spending. But primary care is only half the equation. The other half is where corruption has gone unchecked for decades, hospitals.

The astronomical cost of hospital services is as predatory as the insurance system.

$1,000 to register at the ER. $25,000 for a 1-hour surgery. $150 for a single dose of Tylenol

This isn't healthcare, it's a shakedown. Hospitals claim these inflated prices are necessary to compensate for unpaid bills, but the truth is clear: the entire system is rigged to extract maximum dollars from insurance companies, taxpayers, and patients alike. Insurance companies delay payments and manipulate reimbursements. Hospitals respond by inflating prices. Insurance negotiates them down. The uninsured? They get crushed. This game of pricing warfare feeds the cycle of inflation, and the American people lose, every time. By removing insurance from primary care, HCM eliminates one of the biggest cost drivers. But to fix the system fully, hospitals must follow suit, transitioning to a direct-pay membership model that mirrors what works in primary care. Every citizen would carry a major medical rider alongside their membership. This covers hospitalizations and catastrophic care. If someone can't afford it, their state covers it. The burden of unpaid care is eliminated.

Eliminating the "Uninsured" Excuse

The number one justification hospitals give for outrageous prices is uncompensated care for the uninsured. But under HCM, no one is uninsured. Every American has a membership, and every membership includes a hospital rider. No more billing chaos. No more government bailouts. No more excuses to gouge patients. This system ensures that hospitals get paid, patients get care, and no one goes bankrupt from a hospital visit again.

Breaking Down the Numbers: A System That Works

Let's run the math:

- $150/month for primary care
- $100/month for major medical and prescriptions
- $250/month per citizen-estimated total

With 350 million people in the U.S., that totals $1 trillion per year, a 75% reduction from the current $4+ trillion system. Now divide that responsibility, if 50% of Americans self-pay, the government only funds the other half.

$1 trillion ÷ 2 = $500 billion

$500 billion ÷ 50 states = $10 billion per state annually

That's a fraction of what each state already spends on Medicaid, public health programs, and federal healthcare contributions. The numbers add up. The model is not only plausible, it's preferable.

A Constitutional, Free-Market Solution

Healthcare is not a constitutional right. But as the most powerful and resource-rich nation on Earth, we have a moral obligation and the means to provide a functional, private-sector system that serves everyone.

Healthcare governance belongs to the states, not Washington, D.C.

The free market, not federal mandates, should determine costs.

Doctors, not insurance executives, should direct patient care.

The HCM model achieves all of this, without a single dollar of new taxes and without ceding an inch more power to the corrupt federal machine. And that is why the healthcare membership isn't just a reform. It's a healthcare revolution. It doesn't just fix the system, it takes it back. Back from the bureaucrats. Back from the lobbyists. Back from the predatory insurance-industrial complex that has profited off our pain for decades. The future of healthcare belongs to the people. And with this plan, that future starts now.

The Political Racket Behind America's Healthcare Crisis

Let's be brutally honest: both political parties have sold the American people out. The Republican and Democratic establishments are not opponents, they're business partners. And the business is corruption. The healthcare system has become a cash cow for the elites, and both parties are in on the grift. Insurance conglomerates, Big Pharma, and hospital networks own Washington, D.C. The politicians they bankroll don't represent the people, they protect the system. And that system is bleeding the American people dry. They've leveraged their offices for profit while Americans are crushed by rising premiums, sky-high hospital bills, and deadly delays in care. This isn't just economic theft, it's medical tyranny. Divide, distract, and profit, the agenda is clear; divide the people, distract the public, and loot the nation. While Americans argue over political slogans, party lines, and manufactured outrage, the elites continue siphoning trillions away from America's economy.

It's not about Left or Right. It's about Power vs. the People.

Obamacare: The Trojan Horse for Government-Controlled Healthcare

Healthcare is now over one-third of the federal budget, with more than $4 trillion flowing through the system annually. So, it should come as no surprise that those in power fought to seize control of that cash flow. That's what Obamacare was always about, consolidating healthcare under federal control, not improving care or reducing costs. The Affordable Care Act (ACA) was never designed to make healthcare affordable. It was designed to force Americans into dependency on government-run coverage, expand the role of the federal government in private medical decisions, and push the country toward a single-payer socialist healthcare system. The ACA wasn't just flawed policy, it was a constitutional fraud. According to Article I, Section 7 of the Constitution, all revenue-raising legislation must originate in the House. Yet, Obamacare originated in the Senate, under then-Majority Leader Harry Reid, who hijacked an unrelated House bill and rewrote it wholesale to ram the ACA through without proper constitutional process. Republican leaders knew this and they let it happen. John Boehner, then House Minority Leader, did nothing to defend his chamber's constitutional authority. Nancy Pelosi let Harry Reid strip the House of its power. And the entire Republican establishment, while posturing against Obamacare publicly, stood down when it mattered most. Why? Because they are just as compromised as the Democrats. Both parties benefit from the system. Both take money from the same lobbyists. Both have built political careers on the backs of the American taxpayer while shielding the insurance-industrial complex from any meaningful reform. This is why the Revolution Blueprint is about more than just healthcare reform, it's about reclaiming our entire government. Because nothing will change until the corrupt political class is removed from power. The

Healthcare Membership Model (HCM) is the only viable alternative to the bloated, bureaucratic disaster we have today. It is a common-sense, free market, constitutionally aligned system that restores healthcare to the people by:

- Eliminating the insurance monopoly over primary care
- Dismantling bureaucratic price inflation across hospital networks
- Reducing national healthcare spending by 75%
- Restoring real competition and physician autonomy
- Ending federal overreach and returning control to the states

We're at a crossroads, this system we live under is unsustainable. We face a choice, liberty or control. Either we take back our government, Restore constitutional rule, Reclaim our healthcare system from the grip of corporate and political predators, or we continue down the road toward totalitarianism, where your care, your health, and your future are owned by the state. The time to choose is now, the time to act is here.

The Legislative Betrayal of Obamacare: A Failure of the People

The legislative history of Obamacare is more than a policy failure, it is a constitutional crisis and a reflection of how far we, as a nation, have drifted from the principles of liberty, accountability, and the rule of law. It stands as a blatant betrayal by our government, and by ourselves. As citizens of the United States, we are not mere spectators. We are the final guardians of the Constitution, and we failed to act when it mattered most. While corrupt politicians conspired to hijack one-sixth of the U.S. economy, the American people were divided, distracted, and derailed by partisan theatrics. We watched tyranny unfold and did nothing.

The Constitution: Our Forgotten Shield Against Tyranny

What made America great was never the people in office. It was the system that bound them to law, a system grounded in the

Declaration of Independence and the Constitution of the United States. These founding documents were designed to keep government in check and preserve the people's power. But they only work if we use them. We were never meant to trust government, we were meant to restrain it. That's why Article I, Section 7 exists: to prevent any branch of government from unilaterally imposing taxation without proper, people-driven representation through the House. And that is exactly where Obamacare violated the very core of our constitutional design. Obamacare was the progressive blueprint for medical tyranny. The passage of Obamacare didn't just disrupt the healthcare system, it laid the foundation for a federal takeover of medicine and an explosion of government power. Tens of millions faced skyrocketing premiums and deductibles. Millions lost plans they were promised they could keep. Small businesses were crippled under regulatory pressure. Access to quality care deteriorated as bureaucracy swelled. And worse, it set the precedent for medical authoritarianism that came to fruition during the COVID-19 pandemic:

- Forced vaccinations Mandated lockdowns
- Government censorship of doctors
- Unelected bureaucrats overriding licensed physicians

All of it was made possible because of the precedent set by Obamacare, and our collective failure to stop it when we had the chance. Here's What Actually Happened; Obamacare was a revenue-raising bill, it imposed taxes, penalties, and mandates. But it did not originate in the House. Instead, then-Senate Majority Leader Harry Reid hijacked an unrelated House bill, H.R. 3590, originally titled the Service Members Home Ownership Tax Act of 2009 and gutted it entirely. He replaced it with the full text of the Affordable Care Act and falsely claimed it originated in the House. That was a direct violation of the Origination Clause, one of the most blatant constitutional violations in modern American history.

The Constitution is clear: "All bills for raising revenue shall originate in the House of Representatives." — Article I, Section 7

This was not just a Democrat-led fraud. Republicans were complicit. Speaker Nancy Pelosi surrendered her chamber's authority to the Senate. Republican House Minority Leader John Boehner did nothing to challenge the procedural illegality. After gaining control of the House in 2010, Republicans still refused to use the power of the purse to defund, repeal, or constitutionally challenge the law. Whether through cowardice or collusion, both parties protected the law and betrayed the people.

The Supreme Court's Role in The Nation's Betrayal: NFIB v. Sebelius

In 2012, the Supreme Court heard the constitutional challenge to Obamacare in National Federation of Independent Business v. Sebelius. The core question:

Can Congress force Americans to purchase insurance under the Commerce Clause? The Court answered correctly, Congress cannot compel commerce. But then, in a stunning betrayal of logic and law, Chief Justice John Roberts rewrote the statute mid-ruling, declaring the individual mandate was not a penalty but a tax. This allowed the law to survive under Congress's taxing authority. Yet even under this redefinition, the law should have been struck down. Given it was a tax, then it was an unconstitutional tax, because it originated in the Senate, not the House.

Roberts' manipulation was a constitutional disgrace. He ignored, that Obama and Democrats publicly denied the mandate was a tax. That if it were a tax, it violated the Origination Clause. This ruling was not justice, it was preservation of the political establishment. Obamacare was passed through procedural fraud, the evidence is irrefutable. The entire legislative process was a charade. H.R. 3590 had nothing to do with healthcare, it was a veterans' housing tax bill. The Senate hijacked it, gutted its content, inserted the ACA, changed the title, and passed it. The House never drafted or debated the ACA, nor did it follow proper committee procedure. The Senate passed the bill before the House even saw it. This was legislative fraud, plain and simple. The Senate cannot hijack a House bill and call it "originated in the House." If that process is allowed to stand, the Origination Clause is meaningless, and the people lose their only constitutional control over taxation.

Why didn't they just use the House's original healthcare bill (H.R. 3962) and go to conference committee? Because they would have lost. Republican Scott Brown had just won a special election in Massachusetts, breaking the Democrats' filibuster-proof majority. So instead of negotiating, Obama, Reid, and Pelosi rammed the Senate's fraudulent version through without a single amendment, forcing the House to rubber-stamp a bill it never authored or even had the time to read before casting a vote. This wasn't a legislative error, it was a premeditated conspiracy to bypass the Constitution. Where Was the Republican Party? The Republican establishment had every legal tool available to stop this. John Boehner, as Speaker of the House, could have challenged the bill's constitutional validity. The GOP-controlled House could have refused to fund it, defunded its enforcement, or demanded judicial review. Instead, they caved, again and again. Why? Because both parties serve the same masters. The same lobbyists. The same insurers. The same pharmaceutical giants. This wasn't a Democratic scandal. It was bipartisan collusion to deliver the healthcare industry into the hands of government and global corporate control.

The Way Forward: Challenge Obamacare in Court

Obamacare must be challenged, not just politically, but legally. It is unconstitutional, and that fact must be placed back before the judiciary.

A class-action lawsuit should be filed against the federal government, asserting that:

The ACA violates Article I, Section 7 of the Constitution. Americans were unlawfully taxed under a law that never legally originated. Billions were collected under an invalid statute and must be returned or nullified. Such a challenge would expose the procedural fraud behind the ACA, force the judiciary to confront its own complicity, and open the door to terminating Obamacare once and for all.

What Comes Next: HCM as the Constitutional Alternative

Obamacare must be replaced, not by another federal scheme, but by a constitutional, free-market solution. The Healthcare Membership Model (HCM) returns healthcare to the people and the states. It ends insurance monopolies, bureaucratic interference, and federal overreach. It slashes costs, restores affordability, and empowers patients and doctors. We the People must decide what healthcare looks like in this country, not the politicians, not the insurers, and not the lobbyists.

The Constitution is clear. The path forward is clear.

It's time to fight back and take back what was stolen.

REVOLUTION BLUEPRINT

8

ERADICATING VETERAN HOMELESSNESS

A Moral Imperative and a National Shame

America faces both a moral and economic crisis, one that has been decades in the making. Bad policies, political negligence, and corporate greed have eroded the middle class, leaving hundreds of thousands of citizens without stability or the means to support themselves.

For decades, unprincipled politicians have sent our most honorable, courageous, and selfless citizens to fight unjust wars in foreign lands, asking them to risk everything in service to their country. Yet, when these warriors return home, having served with honor and distinction, they are abandoned by the very government that sent them abroad. Betrayed. Forgotten. Discarded.

Many of our veterans have endured severe trauma, physically, mentally, and emotionally. Instead of providing the care, rehabilitation, and reintegration they need to reclaim their lives, our government turns its back on them, forcing them into poverty, despair, and homelessness. The result? Tens of thousands of veterans sleeping on the streets of the wealthiest nation on Earth, a nation they once bled to defend.

The veteran homelessness crisis is not new. The government's failure to care for its veterans dates back to the Vietnam War. I know this firsthand. My father was one of those veterans. He served multiple combat tours in Vietnam, an infantryman who fought honorably and earned two Purple Hearts. He watched his brothers-in-arms die and fell victim to the opioid crisis that plagued so many soldiers deployed in that war. When he returned home, he was not the same man who left.

His PTSD consumed him. He fought to regain his life, but the weight of his trauma dragged him back down time and time again. Eventually, he stopped fighting. He spent the last 25+ years of his life homeless on the streets of Baltimore, battling addiction. The government failed him, and in doing so, it robbed me and my siblings of a father.

My Father's story is not unique, it is one of millions. Millions of veterans. Millions of families. Millions of lives are shattered by a government that chooses to waste resources rather than care for those who have already given so much.

A Real Solution: A Government That Puts Veterans First

This crisis is solvable. It would take only a fraction of the money our government wastes every single year to eradicate veteran homelessness entirely. Under a new government, of the people, by the people, and for the people, we can make this right.

Through our Department of Defense, we shall ensure that no veteran who has served this great nation is ever left without a home, without care, or without hope again. The time for empty promises is over. The time for action is now.

The Plan: A Three-Phase Strategy to Eradicate Veteran Homelessness

Eradicating veteran homelessness requires a structured, disciplined, and effective approach. This mission will be executed in three critical phases:

1. The Purge - Removing veterans from the streets and restoring their dignity.

2. The Train-Up - Rebuilding discipline, purpose, and self-sufficiency.

3. The Assimilation - Reintegrating veterans into society as productive, respected citizens.

The Purge - Restoring Order, Stability, and Pride

Phase One: Establishing secure housing and infrastructure to provide immediate accommodations to house veterans, laying the foundation for long-term rehabilitation and reintegration. The initial goal is to transition every homeless veteran into a structured and stable environment conducive to rebuilding their lives. A critical component of this initiative involves utilizing existing federal properties. The federal government owns approximately 7,697 vacant buildings and an additional 2,265 partially vacant buildings across the nation. These underutilized properties present a unique opportunity to repurpose existing infrastructure to provide immediate shelter and support services for homeless veterans.

Constitutional Considerations, The Property Clause of the U.S. Constitution grants Congress the authority to manage federal properties.

"The Congress shall have Power to dispose of and make all needful Rules and Regulations respecting the Territory or other Property belonging to the United States." This provision empowers the federal government to utilize its properties for public welfare initiatives, such as housing programs for homeless veterans.

Through strategic implementation of repurposing vacant federal buildings, we can

provide immediate shelter, offering safe and stable housing solutions for homeless veterans. Utilizing existing government assets more efficiently, reduces the need for new construction.

Facilitate Rehabilitation: Create environments where veterans can access essential services, including healthcare, counseling, and job training. This approach not only addresses the urgent need for veteran housing but also ensures responsible stewardship of federal properties in alignment with constitutional provisions.

While The Revolution Blueprint calls for the immediate nullification of all federal land overreach, and returning land back to the states, certain federal properties can be repurposed as micro-sized military bases, dedicated exclusively to eradicating veteran homelessness and facilitating veteran rehabilitation. These bases will serve as barracks, where veterans receive proper shelter, care, and structure.

It begins with a symbolic & mental reset. On day one, veterans will shed their past struggles through a symbolic transformation. The Purge Ceremony

A ceremonial burning of their street clothes and possessions will mark the end of their homelessness and the beginning of their new journey.

This act is a declaration, the government stands with them, and they are no longer alone. From this moment forward, they are in a structured rehabilitation program, on the path to reclaiming a respectable life.

Reintroducing Military Structure & Discipline

Veterans will be issued military Physical Training (PT) gear according to their branch of service, Army veterans will receive Army PT gear, Marines will receive Marine PT gear, Airmen and sailors will receive their respective PT gear also according to their branches of service.

Each veteran will also receive full hygiene kits, showers, haircuts, toiletries, and personal care essentials. Assigned living space with a bunk, footlocker, and wardrobe, thus restoring order and stability into their daily lives.

Assigning veterans to branch specific barracks serves to rebuild military brotherhood & identity. Each branch will manage its own barracks, creating an environment familiar to every veteran. Army veterans will reside in Army-led barracks, Marines in Marine-led barracks, and the Air Force and Navy will have their own designated spaces as well.

Why is this important? Every homeless veteran was once a disciplined, squared-away service member, a soldier, Marine, airman, or sailor who took pride in their uniform. Restoring military order will rekindle that pride, reinforcing their sense of identity, purpose, and worth.

Implementing a daily regimen of structure & rehabilitation

Veterans will follow a structured daily routine, designed to restore discipline and productivity. Early wakeups & physical activity instill routine and mental clarity.

One-on-one counseling to address PTSD, mental health challenges, and trauma.

group therapy programs to foster peer-to-peer support, where veterans come together to share experiences, encourage one another, and rebuild resilience through a strong, united network.

Team-building exercises will help veterans to operate as a unit, reinforcing camaraderie and teamwork. Every veteran will push forward together, overcoming obstacles as a unit and progressing to the next phase only when they are ready.

Command & Leadership: Military-Led Rehabilitation

Active-duty personnel will be assigned to oversee these rehabilitation facilities.

A ranking officer and senior NCO will maintain command and discipline.

The cadre's sole mission will be veteran rehabilitation and reintegration, restoring order, honor, and a sense of purpose to all under their command.

The Goal of the phase one purge is more than just a transition, it is a transformation. Veterans will not just be taken off the streets, they will be given the tools to reclaim their lives.

From homeless to housed, from forgotten to prioritized, from broken to rebuilding. This is the first step toward ending veteran homelessness permanently.

No veteran left behind. No veteran forgotten. The mission starts here.

Phase two is the Train-up, restoring purpose, and rebuilding futures.

The Train-Up phase is where veterans reclaim their sense of purpose and begin the journey toward sustainable, long-term employment. This phase is about discovery, development, and direction identifying each veteran's skills, talents, and potential career paths while providing the necessary training and resources to ensure they reintegrate into the workforce with confidence.

Assessing Skills & Matching Career Paths

The Department of Defense (DoD) will conduct comprehensive skills assessments to determine each veteran's aptitudes, experiences, and interests.

Training opportunities will be evaluated within the DoD, contracts with private sector vendors will ensure access to cutting-edge job training in high-demand career fields. The location of Phase Two training barracks will be strategically chosen to align with the best available employment and training opportunities.

Housing & Transition to Civilian Life Veterans will progress from traditional military-style barracks into transitional housing, designed to strike a balance between structure and independence.

Personalized Living Spaces - Each veteran will be assigned a private room equipped with, a bed, wardrobe, and footlocker. A small TV and computer desk to encourage independent learning and communication while also reinforcing personal space and self-sufficiency.

Technology & Connectivity

Veterans will be issued a laptop and a smartphone to access training resources and job applications. Three sets of civilian clothing to help transition from military to civilian identity.

This carefully designed environment allows veterans to maintain military discipline and pride while gradually reintegrating into civilian life with the support of their military community.

Comprehensive Career Preparation.

Veterans will receive one-on-one assistance with resume building, digital literacy, and professional development. Setting up email accounts and navigating online job platforms.

Mastering Modern Workplace Technology & Career Placement

Cadre will provide hands-on guidance ensuring each veteran is fully prepared for the modern job market, they will receive comprehensive training in workplace technology, equipping them with the digital skills necessary to thrive in today's economy.

Cadre will help veterans navigate the job application process assisting with resume building, cover letters, and online job platforms.

The NVLB initiative will form a network of veteran-friendly employers, partnering with companies throughout the country committed to hiring and supporting former service members. Thus, ensuring job placement in sustainable careers, matching veterans with employment opportunities that align with their skills, training, and long-term goals.

Graduation & Transition to Phase Three

Once a veteran successfully completes career training and secures employment, they will graduate from the program and transition into Phase Three housing, marking their full reintegration into civilian life with independence, stability, and dignity.

Upon graduation, the veteran will move from the training barracks into Phase Three housing centers, strategically located near their new place of employment, ensuring a smooth transition into independent living while maintaining access to their support network.

Why the NVLB initiative works

It creates a structured path from homelessness to self-sufficiency.

It restores confidence, discipline, and a sense of purpose.

It provides real-world job training and direct employment opportunities.

It ensures every veteran transitions into a civilian role with dignity and support.

This phase is more than just job training, it is about rebuilding lives, restoring independence, and ensuring no veteran is left behind.

Phase Three is Assimilation, the final step to independence.

The assimilation phase is the final chapter in the mission to restore dignity, stability, and self-sufficiency to our veterans. By this stage, each veteran has secured stable employment and is ready to fully reintegrate into civilian life with a home of their own.

Permanent Housing: Affordable & Sustainable

Veterans will transition into permanent housing units, converted buildings redesigned into one-bedroom apartments.

These housing complexes will be:

Strategically located in regions with high-demand job markets, ensuring accessibility to employment opportunities.

Affordable, with rent set at a sustainable rate that covers building maintenance, eliminating long-term reliance on federal funding.

Veteran-operated, where resident veterans will be employed in maintenance and operational roles, creating a self-sufficient housing community.

Designed for long-term stability, providing veterans with a safe, structured, and independent living environment.

Continued Support: A Lifelong Safety Net

The No Veteran Left Behind initiative will not abandon veterans once they transition to independent living, it remains a lifelong support system.

Celebrating Their Success - Veterans who have completed the program will be recognized for their resilience and achievement.

Ongoing Support & Mentorship - NVLB will always be accessible to provide:

Encouragement and career guidance.

Networking opportunities and professional development.

Mental health support and community engagement.

Lastly, The NVLB initiative will remain a safety net for those in need If ever a veteran faces setbacks, whether financial, emotional, or professional, NVLB will offer remedial training, job placement assistance, or rehabilitation services to get them back on track.

Honoring Their Sacrifice with Action

The NVLB initiative isn't charity, it's justice. Our veterans have given everything to protect this nation. They deserve more than words, they deserve action.

They served us, now we serve them. They fought for our freedom, now we fight for their future.They gave their all, now we ensure they never struggle alone.

This mission is non-negotiable. No veteran should ever be homeless in the country they defended. We will fix this. And we will do it right.

A Call to Action: Ensuring No Veteran is Left Behind

The No Veteran Left Behind (NVLB) Initiative demands action at the highest levels of government, specifically, from the Department of Defense (DoD). However, achieving this requires legislative approval, which would mean Congress must pass a bill and the President must sign the bill into law.

The Reality: Congress has consistently failed our veterans.

For decades, both political parties, Democrats and Republicans, have demonstrated a shameful, bipartisan legacy of neglect toward those who have served. Veteran homelessness, inadequate healthcare, and systemic inaction are direct results of this Washington establishment's America-last agenda.

Executive Authority & The Fight Ahead

While Congress refuses to act, the President has the executive power to influence defense policy. An executive order could redirect existing funds within the defense budget to implement the NVLB initiative. However, congress could challenge the President's authority in court, using the judiciary as a weapon to block this effort.

The permanent Washington bureaucracy, deeply entrenched in an America-last agenda would resist any move that prioritizes veterans over their own self-serving interests.

This is the harsh truth; Our veterans will never be a priority under the corrupt establishment in Washington. The Need for an America-First Government has never been clearer. There is only one path forward, a government that truly serves the people.

President Trump remains the only leader who has demonstrated real dedication to fixing the veteran crisis. But even with a willing President, Washington's corrupt machine will resist every step of the way. Deploying this plan through the DoD is only possible under a POTUS who prioritizes America first.

Several decades of electing Democrats and Republicans has taught us a hard lesson, our government does not serve us. Our veterans are suffering because these two parties have consistently put them last.

The Solution: The People Take Back Their Country

The only way to guarantee the success of the No Veteran Left Behind Initiative is through the direct intervention of the people. We must reclaim our government and establish a new, America-First leadership, a government of the people, by the people, and for the people.

When We Stand United – WE WIN!!!

God bless our veterans. God bless the America First movement.

RED, WHITE, AND BLACK
A PATH TO PROMISE

For nearly four centuries, Black Americans have carried the heaviest burden ever placed on a people, stripped of their names, land, language, and history yet they remain at the center of morality to a nation that has betrayed them at every turn. Their experience is not just a story of injustice, it is a revelation of identity, purpose, and prophecy. Black America is not a footnote in the American saga; it is the key to its redemption.

A Promise Once Denied

The American experiment has long claimed liberty, justice, and equality as its founding promises. But for Black Americans, these promises have been deliberately withheld. For 360 of their 400 years in this land, Black people have endured slavery, lynching, segregation, redlining, medical experimentation, mass incarceration, and systemic disenfranchisement. These were not anomalies. They were policies, crafted, enforced, and protected by the very government sworn to defend the rights of all. But the oppression of Black America is not merely political or racial. Could it be that it is spiritual? What if Black Americans are the true descendants of Israel?   What if the African slaves brought to the Americas were not just a displaced people, but a divinely marked people, the true descendants of the ancient Hebrews? Historical and cultural parallels strongly support this idea. The original Israelites were a melanated people who practiced oral traditions, lived under covenant law, and were scattered and enslaved when they broke that covenant. From the brutal transatlantic slave trade to the systematic stripping of language, culture, and identity, the experience of African slaves mirrors the prophetic warnings found in Deuteronomy 28. Anthropological and linguistic evidence shows strong links between West African tribes, such as the Igbo and the Ashanti, and ancient Hebraic customs. Some practiced circumcision, observed Sabbath rest, and held oral traditions that trace back to Hebrew lineage. These are not coincidences, they are echoes of a stolen identity.

DNA studies have even identified certain genetic markers linking some African Americans with the Levant, and historical writings from Jewish scholars such as Eldad Ha-Dani (9th century) acknowledge that members of the lost tribes were located in parts of Africa. What if the slaves brought to America were, in fact, those lost tribes, scattered among nations as prophesied?

If this is true, then every policy designed to destroy Black identity, every whipping post, every burning cross, every redlined neighborhood, every falsehood taught in school, is not just racism, but a direct attack on God's covenant people. That would mean the stakes are not only historical or political, but they are also in fact prophetic.

Scripture prophesied of a people who would be enslaved and afflicted in a land not their own for 400 years:

"And he said unto Abram, Know of a surety that thy seed shall be a stranger in a land that is not theirs, and shall serve them; and they shall afflict them four hundred years." Genesis 15:13

That prophecy does not align with modern-day Israel or European Jewry. It aligns with the descendants of those brought to the Americas through the transatlantic slave trade. Deuteronomy 28 describes in painful accuracy the conditions that would befall the true Israelites if they broke covenant with the Most High:

"And the LORD shall bring thee into Egypt again with ships... and there ye shall be sold unto your enemies for bondmen and bondwomen, and no man shall buy you." Deuteronomy 28:68

The only people in human history who were taken into slavery by ships and sold into bondage with no redeemer are Black Americans. This is not coincidence, it is confirmation. The curses of Deuteronomy did not fall on those believed by the world to be God's chosen people. Revelation 2:9 exposes the deception:

"I know thy works, and tribulation, and poverty, (but thou art rich) and I know the blasphemy of them which say they are Jews, and are not, but are the synagogue of Satan."

Those who occupy the land of Israel today do not fit the prophecies of return, nor the identity of the chosen. Could it be they are impostors, assuming the birthright of a people they've long conspired to destroy?

What if the government's betrayal is spiritual warfare?

The United States government, far from being a protector of liberty, has become an instrument of global control. Its allegiance is not to its citizens, but to Israel. This is not speculation, it is geopolitical fact. Billions of U.S. taxpayer dollars are sent to Israel every year, while American cities, especially those populated by Black Americans, are left in ruin. This isn't just about foreign policy. It's about spiritual warfare. Israel, led by those who claim Jewish identity yet fit the description in Revelation 2:9, is actively advancing an agenda of global control, transgender ideology, economic exploitation, and political subversion. This same agenda is used to suppress the awakening of Black Americans, because the elites controlling Isreal are confronted by scripture, they know the truth, Black Americans are the real descendants of Israel. Every injustice committed against them, from forced sterilizations and mass incarceration to poverty and miseducation, is a strategic effort to keep them blind to their true identity. Because if the true children of Israel awaken, the entire system built by impostors will collapse.

Many Americans believe urban decay is part of coordinated plan. Look closely at America's cities. Crime is rampant. Infrastructure is collapsing. Schools are failing. Violence goes unprosecuted. Repeat offenders are returned to the streets. The chaos is not accidental, it is allowed. Now consider who governs nearly every major American city: the Democratic Party. Not only do they control the city governments, but many of the surrounding sister counties as well. Yet, the contrast is striking. In counties with significantly higher white populations, the schools function, the children excel, and the communities are safe. Black students in those counties achieve far better outcomes than their peers in city schools. Is it not fair to ask: Why do Democrats, who govern both the cities and their neighboring counties, allow urban schools to fail so miserably when they clearly know how to produce better results just a few miles away?

These are not just systemic failures. They are intentional strategies of containment and destruction. Urban decay helps maintain dependence, suppresses potential, and discourages unity. It also keeps Black Americans from discovering who they truly are.

Another fair question: Why does the U.S. government prioritize Israel at every turn, even when it conflicts with the needs of American citizens? The answer lies in control. The American Israel Public Affairs Committee (AIPAC) is the most powerful foreign lobbying entity in Washington. It funds candidates, controls narratives, and dictates policy. Few in Congress dare oppose it. Why? Because many of them owe their political careers to AIPAC's support or fear its retaliation.

Worse still, a troubling number of U.S. officials elected, appointed, and agency-embedded hold dual citizenship with Israel. This split loyalty is not just dangerous, it is unconstitutional in spirit. It has been happening for several decades and has gone largely unchallenged. How can a government honor its oath to its constitution and best serve its people when so many of its decision makers serve another nation?

Israel's century's long influence over American foreign and domestic policy is so deeply entrenched that it raises the inevitable question: What if Israel, through its agents and allies in government, has guided the policies that have systematically oppressed Black Americans, specifically to prevent the awakening of the true chosen people?

What if 90% of the Black experience in America's was engineered oppression? Consider this: for over 90% of Black Americans' time in this country, they have lived under sanctioned oppression. From 1619 to the Civil Rights Act of 1964, Black people were either enslaved, segregated, or legally discriminated against. And even after legal barriers were lifted, new ones, economic, judicial, and institutional, were erected in their place. They were denied land after emancipation. Denied GI Bills after WWII. Denied fair housing loans. Denied fair trials. Denied access to quality education. From the Tuskegee syphilis experiments to the crack epidemic to mass incarceration, Black Americans have been targeted for destruction and disintegration.

What if all this wasn't just America's sin but Israel's strategy? Consider the global intelligence sharing, military cooperation, and surveillance systems developed between the U.S. and Israel. The two governments work closely to craft America's foreign and domestic policies. Israel profits from American aid, while Black communities are intentionally left to crumble into chaos and decay from those bad policies and lack of investment.

If Black Americans are the true Israelites, then the war against them has been global, and the beneficiaries of their suppression are the impostors who now occupy their identity and control American policy. The suffering was not just historical injustice, it was a campaign of identity erasure. The Constitution, inspired by higher principles, was designed to protect individual liberty. But in practice, it has been selectively enforced, weaponized against Blacks while protecting all others. Slavery was codified in the founding documents. Jim Crow was protected by the courts. Police brutality is shielded by qualified immunity. These violations are not failures of the system, they are the system operating exactly as designed. What we face is not simply racism. It is a betrayal of divine purpose and a war against the true elect of God.

The Prophetic Call to Rise.

African Descendents are not just victims of history. They are heirs of prophecy.

"Ye are the children of the prophets, and of the covenant which God made with our fathers..." Acts 3:25

This is not a time to beg for rights from corrupt institutions. It is a time to rise in righteousness, reclaim identity, and lead a movement of restoration, spiritually, politically, and constitutionally. The awakening of Black America is the linchpin for national redemption. To restore America to its founding principles, we must first liberate the people it was built upon enslaving. Reclaiming the Republic is not about partisan reform, it's about enforcing the Constitution and fulfilling divine prophecy.

It means

Exposing the impostors who control global finance, media, and government. Rejecting the two-party system, which has conspired to suppress truth. Reinvesting in Black communities, with resources, land, and autonomy. Removing corrupt judges and prosecutors, restoring justice based on law, not politics. Returning to local governance, ending federal overreach, and restoring state sovereignty.

Black and White: United Against Tyranny

What if the one thing the global elite fear most is Black and White united in truth? This movement is not only for Black Americans, but also for all Americans. White America, too, has been betrayed by the same corrupt system. Their children, too, are burdened by endless wars, poisoned by cultural decay, and robbed by globalist policies that serve Israel's interests over our own. Now is the time for White America to break free from the propaganda that has been fed to us for over a century, propaganda designed to sow division, stir resentment, and keep us at odds. The media and government have manipulated our perceptions to prevent unity between Black and White, because they fear what we might accomplish together. This is not the moment to fixate on the surface symptoms of Black oppression. It is the moment to understand the depth of the Black experience. Walk, if only in thought, through the 400-year journey Black Americans have endured, a journey marked by bondage, deprivation, and systemic betrayal.

Empathy begins where judgment ends. And understanding begins with acknowledging one simple truth: this nation was built on a promise, yet for Black America, that promise was denied. The awakening of Black America will inspire White America to join this cause, not as rivals, but as allies. United, we can reclaim this Republic and restore a government that serves the people, not foreign powers or impostor elites. This unity is not only possible, but also essential. The two-party system has long worked to divide the people by race, class, and creed. But the time has come to reject the artificial divisions and recognize that our true enemy is the same, the synagogue of Satan, the impostors who have hijacked our institutions and profited from our suffering. Together, Black, White, and every patriot awakened to truth, we will reclaim our Republic through liberation.

A Glimpse of Liberation: What Awaits Black America What if liberation for Black America wasn't just freedom from oppression, but a divine restoration of identity, dignity, and dominion? Imagine the beauty of rebuilding our cities with resources flowing into the hands of those who've long been robbed. Imagine young Black children growing up in communities filled with pride, knowledge, and purpose, where their history is taught not as tragedy, but as destiny. Imagine schools where excellence is expected, businesses where ownership is standard, and communities where fathers, mothers, and leaders rise in strength, not survive in struggle.

Liberation means no longer begging a broken system for crumbs. It means governing our own communities, reclaiming our own story, and walking in the truth of who you are: God's chosen people, awake and unshackled. This is not fantasy, it is the future awaiting those bold enough to rise together and claim it!

A Word to Christians: Supporting Truth Does Not Betray Faith.

To those in the Christian faith, it is essential to confront this truth with spiritual maturity and scriptural clarity. Coming to terms with the fact that modern Israel may not represent the true chosen people of God does not mean we are abandoning our biblical responsibilities or turning our backs on Israel. In fact, quite the opposite is true. As believers in Christ, our allegiance is not to earthly governments or political institutions, it is to Jesus Christ, the Way, the Truth, and the Life (John 14:6). Our loyalty is to God's eternal Word, not to corrupted regimes who cloak their deeds in religious symbolism. The modern state of Israel, as it exists today, is not above rebuke. Scripture does not call us to support evil simply because it happens to sit on holy ground. It calls us to oppose the works of darkness wherever they appear (Ephesians 5:11). If the government that controls modern-day Israel is led by those who fit the description of the "synagogue of Satan" (Revelation 2:9), then as Christians, we are not betraying God's people by opposing them, we are fulfilling our prophetic duty to expose and confront evil in defense of truth. This is no different from the way the world views America. The nations may detest us for the wars, corruption, and immorality spread under the banner of our government, but that is not a reflection of the American people, many of whom seek peace, justice, and righteousness. Likewise, our stance is not against Israel as a land or a people, but against the corrupt forces controlling it, often with deep ties to our own government, manipulating both for profit and power.

Christians must understand that the Temple was prophesied to be destroyed (Matthew 24:2), and it will be rebuilt, but not by the hands of those who worship power and deception. If Satan has placed his agents at the helm of what should be the most sacred land on Earth, then we are not opposing prophecy by exposing them, we are fulfilling it. Supporting Israel does not mean supporting corruption. Just as opposing America's corrupt leadership is an act of patriotism, opposing the corruption within Israel is an act of obedience to God. Satan must not be allowed to rule over the Holy Land. The synagogue of Satan must be torn down, not with violence, but with truth, faith, and the power of the Word.

This is the test of our time: Will Christians blindly support deception, or will they rise as true witnesses to the light? We stand not against Israel, we stand for the truth. And in doing so, we defend the covenant, the prophecy, and the name of the Most High God.

The Time Is Now

To every Black man reading this: You are not lost. You are not powerless. You are not forgotten. Scripture prophetically proves that you are the sons of Jacob. The priests of the Most High. The warriors of prophecy. You were chosen to endure but also chosen to lead. Chosen to suffer but also chosen to restore.

As Isaiah declared:

"Ye are my witnesses, saith the LORD, and my servant whom I have chosen." Isaiah 43:10

The enemy has tried to erase your identity, imprison your body, and corrupt your mind, but your spirit remains unbroken. Your call is not just to protest, but to govern. To rebuild what was torn down. To restore the Republic and usher in a new era of righteousness.

Let the fake crumble. Let the lies collapse. Let truth rise.

From the Promise Denied to the Promise Fulfilled, the Kingdom will Rise Through Red, White, and Black.

www.ingramcontent.com/pod-product-compliance
Lightning Source LLC
Chambersburg PA
CBHW050218270326
41914CB00003BA/463